T0196405

Where Is
God
in the
Turmoil
of a
Life-Threatening
ILLNESS?

Karen Haren and
Sue L. Frymark

WESTBOW
PRESS®
A DIVISION OF THOMAS NELSON
& ZONDERVAN

This book is a work of non-fiction. Unless otherwise noted, the author and the publisher make no explicit guarantees as to the accuracy of the information contained in this book and in some cases, names of people and places have been altered to protect their privacy.

WestBow Press books may be ordered through booksellers or by contacting:

WestBow Press
A Division of Thomas Nelson & Zondervan
1663 Liberty Drive
Bloomington, IN 47403
www.westbowpress.com
844-714-3454

Because of the dynamic nature of the Internet, any web addresses or links contained in this book may have changed since publication and may no longer be valid. The views expressed in this work are solely those of the author and do not necessarily reflect the views of the publisher, and the publisher hereby disclaims any responsibility for them.

Any people depicted in stock imagery provided by Getty Images are models, and such images are being used for illustrative purposes only.
Certain stock imagery © Getty Images.

Scripture quotations marked NLT are taken from the Holy Bible, New Living Translation, Copyright © 1996, 2004, 2015 by Tyndale House Foundation. Used by permission of Tyndale House Publishers, Inc., Carol Stream, Illinois 60188. All rights reserved.

Scripture quotations marked KJV are taken from the King James Version.

Scripture quotations marked NIV are taken from The Holy Bible, New International Version®, NIV® Copyright © 1973, 1978, 1984, 2011 by Biblica, Inc.® Used by permission. All rights reserved worldwide.

Scripture quotations marked TLB are taken from The Living Bible, copyright © 1971 by Tyndale House Foundation. Used by permission of Tyndale House Publishers Inc., Carol Stream, Illinois 60188. All rights reserved. The Living Bible, TLB, and the The Living Bible logo are registered trademarks of Tyndale House Publishers.

ISBN: 978-1-6642-0116-3 (sc)
ISBN: 978-1-6642-0115-6 (hc)
ISBN: 978-1-6642-0117-0 (e)

Library of Congress Control Number: 2020914619

Print information available on the last page.

WestBow Press rev. date: 09/25/2020

Dedicated to all those who attended our classes and gave us so much insight into the experience of living with a life-threatening illness.

Shining the light of Christ through the dark times of a life-threatening illness.

CONTENTS

PREFACE

Coauthor Karen Haren has lost several family members including her first husband, who died of leukemia, leaving her with three young children. She later found faith in Jesus Christ. In 2003, Karen was deeply affected by the death of her father, as she observed the beautiful interactions of her family. During the last days and hours of his life he was surrounded by his children, grandchildren, and his wife. Karen was extremely moved by what she saw as the hand of God orchestrating the events. The distance she felt toward her father, since her adolescence, melted away. She started looking at life in a new light—that God uses the end of life for especially important purposes.

They named the ministry Wilderness Journey because, like the Israelites who wandered in the wilderness for forty years, people can feel lost without a clear path when they are going through this kind of experience. Not only is there a need for support, there is a need for spiritual comforting. In their anguish, people often want to know where God is in this turmoil. He is in the middle of the storm, knocking at the door, waiting for us to open our hearts to Him. He comes to us in His Word and in those surrounding us, waiting to help us. People need to hear the Christian message when they need it most—when they are facing death.

Sue Frymark, coauthor and a lifelong Christian, spent over forty years as a nurse focusing on cancer patients and their families. She often wished she could share the hope she had in Jesus Christ, but workplace evangelizing was not allowed unless the person being served raised the topic. Sue could see the peace in those depending on their faith in Jesus Christ. Through her own mother's story, she saw this as well. She saw how her mother's preparation for her death allowed the family to more freely grieve, knowing her end-of-life decisions had been made. Years later, her family still talks about their mother's beautiful death. In 2015, Sue was diagnosed with a life-threatening illness for which there is no cure. She now has a special understanding for those also traveling this difficult path.

To deliver their message, Sue and Karen developed a nine-week educational support group titled "Help for Families: Facing a Life-Threatening Illness Holding Christ's Hand." They began teaching it in 2010 (see appendix 1).

ACKNOWLEDGMENTS

Thank you to all those who have been helpful in the development of this ministry and this book. There have been so many, including those who reviewed our original manuscript. Specifically, we wish to thank Bonny Groshong for her leadership and support from the very beginning. Other key people include Pastor Kurt Luebkeman, Donanne Bowman, Nancy Espinoza, Vi Hansen, Valerie Thibeau, Ron Drews, the Lutheran Women in Mission, Concordia University, and Kay Kirkbride.

INTRODUCTION

Why is it that we don't want to talk about death and dying? For some it is the fear of the unknown following death. For others it maybe the fear of pain and possible loss of independence. In some cultures, caring for sick or aging family members is just a part of life. It is expected and planned for. However, modern Western families are not usually prepared. Homes are not often designed to accommodate an ill or disabled person; all the adults in the home may have to work, leaving no one to care for someone who is ill; or family members might be geographically dispersed.

In the Bible, the concept of family is much more comprehensive than we think of today. The family, or the tribe, consisted of anyone related or accepted in. It was made up of all the known generations. The tribe established laws and norms in order to maintain a cohesive society. God created inheritance and the passing of blessings to help maintain the family structure through the millennia. It was not only the passing of money and possessions, but included social status and blessings for a long and prosperous life.

We pass along money and property, usually in the form of a will, but our society does not put any real significance into, or build traditions for, the passing of blessings. We have a poor social memory of the family experience of a life-threatening illness.

Gradually, over many decades, Western society has forgotten how to cope with issues related to death and dying. Aware of this, the authors, Karen Haren and Sue Frymark, created Wilderness Journey

Ministries to help individuals and families cope with the spiritual, emotional, and practical difficulties of living with a life-threatening illness.

This book addresses several theological issues from a nondenominational Christian perspective. Most mainstream Christian denominations agree on many foundational tenets. For example, they agree that Jesus Christ is the Son of God, that He died on the cross to save us from our sin, and that God promises to bring us to Heaven if we have accepted Christ as our Savior. Here are the core values of the ministry:

- Jesus is the only Son of God and the only path to salvation.
- A life-threatening illness is a family experience.
- End-of-life planning and discussion should take place early.
- Talking about death will not kill you.
- God values us every moment of our lives.
- God uses the end of life to bring healing, reconciliation, and sometimes salvation.
- We do not lose our purpose and worth in God's eyes when we become sick or incapacitated!

God's love, grace, and mercy are so great that we human beings can hardly understand it. He has open arms for all who will accept Him. It is because of this great love that we have been given gifts to help cope with the turmoil of a life-threatening illness.

1

EMOTIONAL REACTIONS

You keep track of all my sorrows. You have collected all my tears in your bottle. You have recorded each one in your book. (Psalm 56:8 NLT)

We know we will die someday, but it is always a shock to face it when it becomes a reality. The words cancer, Alzheimer's, advanced heart failure, or any life-threatening illness can stop you in your tracks. There may be spiritual turmoil within the family. Questions arise such as: "Why did God let this happen?" "Where is He now?" You may feel angry with God. Though the illness may be treatable for a while, the thought of dying is overwhelming. Perhaps you have been given an estimated time, or you may be facing unpleasant treatment. Hopefully, the disease is one that can be cured, or at least you may expect a time of remission.

In any case, your life has changed. You are on a new journey now. It feels like a solitary journey, but, really, it's not. As John Donne wrote nearly four hundred years ago: "No man is an island unto himself." The Bible doesn't say we will not endure hardship, but it does say God will never leave us or forsake us. We were never meant to walk through life and death alone. This experience will affect everyone who loves you and cares for you. It may affect those who come after you, even for generations.

Living with a life-threatening illness is usually an intense experience. Sometimes emotions can swirl together like an ocean wave, tossing you around and making you feel you are going crazy! This is normal. Lifelong coping mechanisms may suddenly start failing. It is frightening because you have never felt this way before. Identifying the usual causes of common emotions helps to normalize the experience.

Here are some common emotions:

Fear

Fear is probably your first reaction to the news. It can hit you

suddenly, making you feel cold or numb. Sounds may fade away as if you cannot hear very well. Even the thoughts in your mind may be lost. You feel you are in a surreal dream. How do you tell your family, your children, your spouse? And then there's the question of why. It is so unfair. We cry out to God, but we get no answers.

As you come out of the fog, there is a need to regain control. This may happen through telling your medical story or seeking information about your illness, or you might simply be in denial. For some time, you might go about your daily life as usual until the moment the truth strikes you. Initially, you might just want time alone to emotionally grasp the situation before discussing it with others or dealing with their reactions. Some family and friends want to gather during such times. As everyone returns to his or her usual daily routines, there will be quiet times alone.

You may have physical symptoms that limit your ability to carry out some of your family or work duties. Perhaps you may have to reduce your work hours resulting in a reduction of income or a change of insurance benefits. Changes in family roles and differing expectations may occur. Your family members may need to juggle their own schedules to assist you.

> Kay was a forty-one-year-old wife and stay-at-home mother of two small children when she was diagnosed with breast cancer. Her husband and sister went with her for a consultation with the chemotherapist and radiation oncologist, while grandma stayed with the children. Together they were able to get their medical questions answered and were relieved how patient the doctors were. They began to understand the demands of medical procedures and treatments. They left with a list of resource staff and services such as children's counselors, social workers, and a nurse who taught classes about the treatments she would undergo. They went home to meet with friends and family to learn how they might help her with things like driving her to treatments, helping with childcare, and doing regular household chores. Kay was feeling a bit overwhelmed. She thanked everyone for their support but excused herself to read her Bible and pray and just cry. However, she was looking forward to the next day when she would meet with her friend Jane Marie, a breast cancer survivor. Her husband, Frank, felt very comforted knowing his family offered

their support too. He scheduled an appointment to have coffee with his pastor the next day to share his feelings and ask for prayer.

People's lives usually revolve around work, family, church communities, and social activities making up the foundation of their emotional support system. Disrupting this support can have a devastating emotional impact.

Family members and caregivers can have many feelings, such as fear, grief, and guilt but may be more reluctant to express these because of a sense of responsibility and wanting to "be strong" for the ill person. Not everyone in the family will react alike. One person may be overwhelmed with grief, while others feel fear but can function with everyday activities. A teenager may act as if nothing is going on within the family but can be very scared. These different reactions can sometimes create impatience among family members if they are not sensitive to what is going on underneath.

Fear may come and go throughout your illness but is usually the most intense in the beginning. There are a variety of specific fears such as fear of the unknown, of physically being in pain, and of the actual dying process. There can be fear of discussing death, of end-of-life decisions, and fear of being dependent on others. Fear is *not* a sin or sign of weakness. Believers are not immune from the fear of dying. Even Jesus felt fear as He faced His own death. You may be afraid to be afraid! You may fear this is a sign of weakness or lack of faith. You may be afraid that you might be giving in to the disease.

> Fear thou not; for I am with thee be not dismayed;
> for I am thy God: I will strengthen thee; yea, I will
> help thee; yea, I will uphold thee with the right hand
> of my righteousness. (Isaiah 41:10 KJV)

Anger

Anger is a feeling many are afraid to express, and yet it is a normal response. You might feel the situation is unfair. Maybe friends or family have let you down, or medical information is disappointing. Sometimes a person may be afraid of being with someone who is angry, whether it is the ill person or a family member. Just listening to the angry feelings a person expresses will make him or her feel much better. Simply listen and don't try to reason with the person. At times, gently encouraging the person to identify their fears can be helpful. Keep in mind that anger can be a symptom of depression. For the Christian, we may fear that when we are angry with God, He will punish us. However, He knows our feelings, so we might as well acknowledge them to Him. Be honest with God. It is better than turning away from Him.

> Chuck's story. "The doctor came out after operating on my wife and said they could not remove all the cancer. He said it was basically everywhere. She would have six months—maybe a year. I headed for the elevator. The doors closed, and I was alone. I clenched my fists and shook them to the heavens and screamed, 'Why Lord? Why her? She is such a wonderful person!'"

Grief

Grief and loss can be felt by anticipating the separation from loved ones. You may grieve over the need to leave a career or a job you love, or the need to cut back on family activities. You may feel sad when you think about all the family plans, career possibilities, and personal goals that might not become a reality. Eventually, this sadness may subside as a plan of care becomes established, and hope becomes more defined. Don't be afraid to cry. This is the body's natural way to cope by reducing the internal pressure that builds up inside. A support group may also be helpful.

Suicidal feelings

Wishing you could die or having suicidal feelings is not uncommon, especially if the illness is exceedingly difficult. However, it is a warning sign that should never be ignored. *If you are feeling suicidal, tell someone right away!* Although, suicidal feelings usually get better over time, there may be underlying medical, pharmacological, or psychological issues that can be treated. Contact your doctor or family member right away. There is hope.

> Therefore, is my spirit overwhelmed within me; my heart within me is desolate. (Psalm 143:4 KJV)

> God is our refuge and strength, always ready to help in times of trouble. So, we will not fear when earthquakes come and the mountains crumble into the sea. Let the oceans roar and foam. Let the mountains tremble as the waters surge! (Psalm 46:1–3 NLT)

Guilt

Guilt is a difficult emotion often filled with "what ifs." It can stem from anxiety and fears. It can be realistic or, at other times, be unfounded. You may feel guilt for ignoring early symptoms, or you may have had certain life habits—smoking, for example— that contributed to your risk of getting sick. You may feel guilty about becoming a burden, causing emotional pain for the family, or depleting family savings.

Guilt on the part of the family member may be from not seeing symptoms sooner, not being able to help more, or having to make certain medical decisions. There can be unresolved feelings of guilt from the past such as poor life choices, mistakes, or even crimes. The guilt may be from events and decisions from a previous death of a loved one. Sometimes guilt can come from not being able to reconcile a relationship. There are always things we can find in ourselves, or in our past, that cause us guilt. Fortunately, our Lord's grace covers all our sins!

Anxiety

Anxiety is a common response to a serious diagnosis. Often people feel a loss of control. It might seem like the illness is controlling everything—time, relationships, and emotions. This comes because there are so many unknown factors. As details about the illness become clear, the anxiety level may go down. First, it is important for each person to be aware of his or her own signs of stress to recognize when it is becoming impactful. Second, find those interventions that help reduce stress and anxiety for you. These can be in the form of exercise, prayer, journaling, music, talking with others in a support group, or individual counseling.

Needing to go to more and more medical appointments can cause chaos. Interjecting them into an already busy family schedule only adds more stress, especially when school-aged children are involved. As a medical plan of care is agreed upon, and as there is some help with daily life or even being able to go back to work, the loss of control will lessen.

We believe that the end of life is an important time to God. It is part of His plan for humankind—to hold society together, to pass on the blessing from one generation to another, and to create a social conscience about the value of life. He is actively involved. It is His desire to heal and reconcile families. Sometimes He heals the body too. God uses this time to bring us and others closer to Himself. Like the instruments in a symphony that "weave" music together to produce a magnificent sound, God uses many people and circumstances to bring attention to His purposes during this experience. He wants to heal the soul, strengthen families, and bring some to the saving knowledge of Jesus Christ. We call this phenomenon "God's symphony orchestra."

God has a plan for us for every day. He wants each of us to have a good life and death. This is so powerful that we believe that the end of life might be *the most* important time of a person's life. It can be an experience that will change whole families for generations. God uses the end of life for good. We do not lose our value and worth in His eyes ever, even if we become sick or incapacitated!

> Now to him who is able to do immeasurably more
> than all we ask or imagine, according to his power
> that is at work within us, to him be glory in the
> church and in Christ Jesus throughout all generations,
> for ever and ever! Amen. (Ephesians 3:20–21 NIV)

2

STARTING THE CONVERSATION—
NANCY'S STORY

Starting the conversation—it's not an easy thing to do. I needed to have a conversation with my brother-in-law and sister-in-law. She had just been diagnosed with her third recurrence of breast cancer. And this was not going to be an easy battle. I knew I needed to minister to them, but I didn't feel I had all the tools I wanted to be effective. I was in Oregon, and they were in Colorado. I made several trips there and had many phone conversations. In the beginning, we had several gentle conversations. As time when on, they got deeper and deeper. We discussed my sister-in-law's wishes for her end-of-life care. She wished to remain at home. She had several other desires that were important to her. So, it was especially important to include her husband, her daughter, and her son. I was able to use the tools I learned in the Wilderness Journey Ministry classes to help guide the conversations and help her feel relaxed. They empowered her to make her wishes known.

Over several months, I made more trips and had more conversations by phone. At times I needed be a mediator and help her express wishes. It wasn't always easy. Part of her family experience was that they weren't ready to let her go. But she was ready. And she  knew how she wanted to do it. My sister-in-law definitely had some opinions and wishes she would hope that her family would adhere to. And I was there to facilitate that. I would fly out to Colorado, with my new-found knowledge, and help them have these discussions. Over time the discussions became easier and easier and the conversations became more meaningful. So, my experience with attending the classes was invaluable. I learned a lot about family dynamics in the end-of-life times. I had experienced three deaths in my own family that really went very well. So, I was not too hesitant to help them through this time.

On one of my visits to Colorado, my sister-in-law gave me permission to investigate some church communities for her and her husband to attend. They had been members of a church in the past but had stopped going on a regular basis. I just knew that a caring community would be so helpful for them in this journey they were on. So, I made a few phone calls, and I found a church community where the pastor seemed so willing to be open and caring and just embraced them at their first Sunday visit. It really was the most significant experience they had together as a couple. To this day, even after my sister-in-law's passing, my brother-in law still attends the same church, is committed to being active in the church, and has found that they have been a great support.

So, having the courage to suggest that they step out and try a church community where they lived was just one of the many blessings that I found through the Wilderness Journey Ministries classes. It enabled me to be bold and look for the opportunities to minister to them. I'm so happy to say that their experience as a family turned out to be incredibly positive. It could have been difficult, but her wishes were respected. Her husband, her daughter, and her son were all involved in her care. She was able to remain at home. Her passing was as uncomplicated as it possibly could have been. I can sincerely say, as a nurse and a cancer survivor myself, that the more tools you have, the more successful the journey. I'm so grateful to have been given the opportunity to attend the classes, get the tools, and put them to use. It enabled me to start the conversation.

3

COPING WITH A LIFE-THREATENING ILLNESS

How can you cope with a serious, life-threatening illness? How can you go on amid the myriad of doctor's appointments, nausea, profound weakness, physical impairment, and the serious disruption to life as you know it?

It is normal if you suddenly cannot find the ability to cope. You may not be able to take care of yourself or your loved one emotionally or physically. There is no shame in this. Unless you are a mechanic, you take your car to a repair shop when it breaks down. You can try, but you probably will not be able to do as well as those who are trained to do the job. A life-threatening illness is complicated because it affects many more areas of our mind and body. You can try to go it alone, but the journey will be harder. If you are independent and private by nature, you may need time to keep this to yourself, but, eventually, reaching out to others will make the experience so much easier. If this is particularly difficult, choose one person to share with only to the extent you feel comfortable. As time goes by, look for others with whom to share.

Your support system

Your family may be your greatest ally. But this is not true for everyone. Some people do not have family; perhaps the family lives far away; or they may not be dependable. Your "family members" don't have to be blood relatives. Good friends, members of groups such as church small groups, a car club, athletic class members, or your own pastor might be like "family" to you. Sometimes, if you see the same people when you go in for chemo, they can become part of your support system.

At times it may be helpful to talk with someone who is not emotionally involved. Many health organizations such as the American Cancer Society, the American Parkinson's Association, or the Alzheimer's Association have volunteers available to listen. There are also support groups at care centers and online. Physicians and their medical team often have good suggestions about this.

Two free and useful communication resources are:

www.caringbridge.org allows people to post pictures and updates to others who have permission to view it like a private Facebook page. Followers are notified by email of a new posting. Friends and families can send comments, prayers, and messages back.

www.carecalendar.org helps by offering a calendar of information of needed help, specifying dates and time frames. It also can list preferred foods or special needs and times when visitors are especially welcome to relieve the family caregiver. Friends and family can post when they can bring a meal, help with driving, schedule a visit, etc. This resource requires someone to set up and do regular updates. It is a perfect way for someone with computer skills to be helpful.

Communicating

In our culture, talking about death is taboo. Many people buy life insurance policies and write wills, but end-of life decisions are just as important. Death can strike anyone anytime. Why are people afraid to talk about death? Even though it is an unpleasant subject, talking about death will not kill you! We are afraid to talk about it for fear it will come true.

It is important for you decide how you want to be treated if you cannot speak for yourself and are in danger of dying. It is helpful to start communicating with others early after you are first diagnosed. The Advance Directive is a document designed to help you tell everyone what kind of medical treatments you want, or don't want. You should review it if you have one or fill one out if you don't. You will need to name the person who will speak for you. The formal name for this person is "the health care representative." Most importantly, talk about this with your family. You will make the decisions in the end, but it will help your family members if you discuss this with them.

This is an important time for listening to one another to understand each person's fears and concerns. There are no right or wrong feelings. It is not a time of reacting to one another's feelings but time to listen. This is a time for family members to develop patience with one another as emotions may run high. Having regular gatherings helps keep issues in check. Try having potlucks, games, or movie nights once a month or more.

We can become anxious and panicky if we experience a new

symptom. We tend to speculate, fearing the worst. Being unclear or uninformed about an issue can lead to confusion and overreacting. It is more helpful to deal with facts and not make any premature assumptions. Most symptoms can be attributed to a variety of medical issues, some easily treatable. It is important to report any new symptom to your medical team, but sometimes we worry about issues that may never arise.

> **Mary and Joe** were a very elderly couple. Mary was recovering from cancer surgery for tumors in her oral cavity. We were all impressed with the clear love between them. Joe's stayed at the hospital as long as he could, sitting by her bedside, until his transportation arrived. On one of my visits I saw Mary alone. She confided in me that she was concerned about Joe's behavior because he never kissed her goodbye, as was their custom. There was an invisible wall between them. Later I was able to speak to Joe privately. I learned Joe was afraid he would hurt her if he kissed her, and second, he thought cancer was contagious. I reassured him with the facts. He was so relieved. The invisible wall went down, and he resumed his affectionate goodbye kisses.

Fear of being negative can be a real issue because everyone is trying so hard to be upbeat. Some family members or friends need to share difficult information. It is important to be realistic but hopeful. The calmer and more matter of fact one can be the more likely the conversation can be successful and meaningful.

Communication can become more difficult due to stress. Emotions can be extremely intense creating impatience and regrettable comments. Or other times we are overprotective. Sometimes we fear being honest might hurt someone or make him or her angry, so we don't share our needs and feelings.

To improve communications, try to avoid using "you" statements such as "You should mow the lawn for Grandma." "You" statements put people on the defense. "I" statements, such as "I need to find someone to mow the lawn for Grandma," can imply needing help solving her problem. "I" statements reduce tension. They are especially effective in seeking help from others whether we are the ill person or a family member.

Christ can bring healing and peace. "Let us fix our eyes on Jesus the author and perfecter of our faith." (Hebrews 12:2 NIV)

> Make allowance for each other's faults and forgive anyone who offends you. Remember, the Lord forgave you, so you must forgive others. Above all, clothe yourselves with love, which binds us all together in perfect harmony. And let the peace that comes from Christ rule in your hearts. For as members of one body you are called to live in peace. And always be thankful. (Colossians 3:13–15 NLT)

Communicating with the memory impaired or person with dementia

It can be a challenge visiting with those experiencing confusion, limited

memory, and loss of words. In addition, they often experience anxiety, agitation, anger, and frustration. Remember it is the disease causing these symptoms interfering with their ability to communicate rather than the persons themselves. Here are some helpful tips:

- Have realistic expectations.
- Keep it short and simple.
- Expect repetition and use repetition.
- Give them time to respond.
- Do not argue or correct.
- Be aware of your body language.
- Touch—Ask for permission. "I'm in the mood for a hug. What about you?" or "I could use a hug. Any chance you could give me one?" "Would you mind if I kiss you on the cheek before I leave?" Then thank them. Let them know they are giving you something.
- Speak slowly, clearly and with eye contact.

Questions can be tricky. Close-ended questions (that can be answered yes or no) are usually better. Ways to say no:

- "I wish I could."
- "Oh, that would be nice."
- "I don't know. I'll see what I can find out."
- "I think it is too cold (hot) today."

Some things to say:

- "Thanks for letting me …"
- "It's nice to see you."
- "Can I visit you again?"
- "I'm going for a walk. Would you like to walk with me?"

Some things *not* to ask or say:

- Ask what they had for lunch.
- Ask what they would like to do.
- Ask, "What is my name?"

- Say, "You just told me that."
- Say, "I already know that."

Singing of old familiar songs and hymns can be a wonderful way to connect, especially if you sing along. Even those who normally can't speak may sing aloud with you.[1]

Talking with someone with dementia should be assessed on a case-by-case basis. To reduce your own stress, have realistic expectations. Keep communication short, and don't be surprised if they repeat themselves or come back to a previous conversation. Try not to correct or argue with them. It can raise anxiety for both of you. Seek other suggestions from the health-care team and community organizations.

Communicating with the health-care system

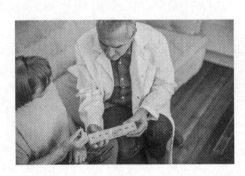

It is important to have a good relationship with your doctor and the health-care team from the first encounter. You need to know it is okay to ask any questions you have. Of course, the physician is the first source for medical questions and information, but others can be helpful too. Information you find on the internet or get from well-meaning friends may not be accurate, so check it out with the medical team. It is beneficial to have someone go along to a medical appointment, especially those where test results are reviewed or a change in the medical care plan is to be discussed. When there is a large family, designate someone, other than the ill person, to be the point person for family members seeking information. Having other resource members or family involved in

---

[1] Contributed by Kay Kirkbride, RN retired.

care in no way takes control away from the ill person. It is up to that person to make the decisions unless they are unable.

Early after the diagnosis, schedule a family conference with the physician and/or health-care team to discuss the diagnosis, prognosis, and treatment care plan for the ill person. A family conference provides an opportunity for all involved family members to hear the same information at the same time and to discuss questions or concerns. Use a list of questions or issues prepared in advance. Request an additional family conference during complex times of treatment when major decisions are being considered. The health insurance companies often have nurses available who follow complex cases. They can seek and advocate for necessary authorizations or benefits. Hospital social workers can also be helpful. It can be overwhelming to work with large organizations, such as insurance companies, hospitals, or state assistance programs. It is helpful to have a social worker or resource person to navigate such groups.

Long-distance caregiving

Caregiving long distance can be challenging, especially if there are no family members locally. This is made easier by modern technology. For example, locating resources such as nursing care, pastoral care, and agencies offering volunteer help can be located on the internet and can do a great deal to help a long-distance loved one. In addition, face-to-face communication is available to nearly everyone with a smart phone or a computer. Long-distance caregiving is defined as the providing support and/or management of the needs of an ill person living more than an hour away. If family meetings are planned, don't forget to include the long-distance caregiver or family member by video chat if possible.

Special communication issues

When problems present themselves, making communicating difficult, it is often a heads-up that outside help is needed or at least can be helpful. For example, how much information should be shared with children, the extremely ill, or elderly persons?

Preexisting family conflicts can surface, especially if they were serious. The onset of a life-threatening disease creates an important opportunity to heal past differences. The earlier conflicts can be resolved, the easier the future path will be. Of course, some wounds cannot be healed with a short conversation. Consider talking to a professional counselor or pastor.

> And hope does not disappoint us, because God has
> poured out his love into our hearts by the Holy Spirit,
> whom he has given us. (Romans 5:5 NIV)

Asking for help

Never assume others know what you need and never assume that if they really cared, you would not have to ask. Be specific as to what assistance you need. Let others help you. This ministers to them as well, by reducing their feelings of helplessness. When asking for help, try to pinpoint the need as much as possible. Here are some common areas of need:

- Help with daily or weekly chores
- Emotional support through visits
- Help with finances or help locating financial assistance
- Babysitting children or picking them up from school

- Walking the dog
- Yard work
- Travel to doctor's appointment
- Grocery shopping and meal preparation

Communication tips from the Bible

Tell the truth in love: "So, stop telling lies. Let us tell our neighbors the truth, for we are all parts of the same body." (Ephesians 4:25 NLT)

Stay current: Don't store up unexpressed feelings and needs and "don't sin by letting anger control you. Don't let the sun go down while you are still angry, for anger gives a foothold to the devil." (Ephesians 4:26–27 NLT)

Don't attack people; attack problems: "Don't use foul or abusive language. Let everything you say be good and helpful, so that your words will be an encouragement to those who hear them." (Ephesians 4:29 NLT)

Act; don't react. Be gentle and forgiving of one another: "Get rid of all bitterness, rage, anger, harsh words, and slander, as well as all types of evil behavior. Instead, be kind to each other, tenderhearted, forgiving one another, just as God through Christ has forgiven you." (Ephesians 4:32 NLT)

4

COME OFTEN, IT HELPS— CATHERINE'S STORY

Catherine and her physician had decided to stop the chemotherapy. She felt that it wasn't controlling her cancer. She seemed withdrawn, and she told us that she had nothing to look forward to but dying painfully back at the nursing home.

Then, in an attempt to break through the wall, she was building around herself, I asked Catherine if she'd like to have a sketch made of herself. One of our volunteers enjoyed doing charcoal portraits for patients.

"No. I don't want a reminder of how awful I look—skinny with no hair," Catherine replied abruptly. Apparently, I'd looked right past my patient's appearance—and underestimated how important it still was to her.

At our weekly cancer rehabilitation team conference, we talked about Catherine and how she was losing her sense of identity and purpose. We resolved to help Catherine set some short-term goals, improve her self-image, and feel a part of something again. Since I knew Catherine best, I made the first move.

I knew that Catherine had brought her wig with her, so I encouraged her to wear it. She said that she'd need a special mirror to style it properly but that she could get a friend to bring it to her. Seeing at least a spark of interest in the idea, I ventured further.

"Catherine, if you wear your wig, why not have the sketch done? If you don't want it, I do. I've come to care for you the way you look now. I'd like that memory in a sketch," I said.

"Oh, is that what this is all about?" she asked with a slight smile. "Well, I'll do it for you, Sue, but it will take a few days to get the mirror." Now we had our short-term goals—get the mirror, style the wig, and have the sketch done. We were on our way.

Nurses urged Catherine to wear her own clothes in the hospital, and the recreational staff helped with her makeup. (The day she died; her nails were still polished.) The physical and occupational therapists got her out of her room and into their departments for a change of scenery.

Thus, the walls around Catherine began to crumble. She spent time with staff on the patio, and she gazed at the mountains from the skybridge. She developed what became a famous twinkle in her eyes. The charcoal sketch was lovely. Catherine had it framed and displayed it in her room for all to see.

Since Catherine had been a beautician, I asked her to teach me some pointers about wigs. She modestly agreed. However, I learned from other team members that Catherine was happily telling them how little I knew about wigs and that she was going to help me. I wanted to spread out a good thing, so we spent several sessions examining free wigs that were provided by the American Cancer Society.

Thus, Catherine became an involved member of the team, as all patients need to be. She socialized with us all and took a renewed interest in her family as well. She showed us photographs of them as if to say, "I'm part of this also." With the help of our recreational therapist, she sent them letters. Simple contact with those she cared about became increasingly important.

Catherine also regained a sense of being part of God's world. Often when patients tell us that they do not want to be visited by clergy or that faith in God is unimportant to them, we drop that option of support. We learned from Catherine that that may change. At first, Catherine was adamant about not wanting to see a member of the clergy. But, on looking back, I realize her response was given during a time of anger when she was asking, "Why me, God?" As time passed, however, and her anger cooled, I learned that one of her sisters was a Catholic nun. I could then discuss with Catherine what her faith had meant to her at one time.

Gradually, Catherine's faith became more and more important. We noticed that she started to wear her rosary. She was embarrassed at first; if we commented, she'd explain she was wearing the rosary because "it matches my outfit." Visits by the Catholic priest and by one of the hospital chaplains became more frequent. One day Catherine told the chaplain that it made no difference to her what religion we each were as "we're all brothers and sisters in Christ." Clearly, Catherine saw herself as part of an even greater whole than before.

More content with herself and her relationship with God, Catherine was able to focus her concerns on the rest of us. She spent time reflecting, with the various people who cared for her, on the memories she shared with them: the wigs, the charcoal sketch, the visits to the skybridge with the physical therapists, and so on. She expressed her love for others by a greeting that radiated from her smile and her eyes.

As Catherine grew weaker, she told us she wanted someone with her so she wouldn't die alone. We took turns sitting with her, and in her final days after her family had arrived, we did so to relieve them. A certain peace began to take over. Catherine told a chaplain that she dreamed she was going through a dark tunnel with someone beside her.

One afternoon while I sat with her, Catherine asked me to pray that the Lord would take her quickly. She told me she was ready to die, and as she spoke, she held one hand to my face, as she often did. As my tears rolled from my cheeks onto Catherine's hand, her physician entered the room.

At first, the physician hesitated, as though he felt he might be intruding, but we beckoned him to enter. When he took Catherine's other hand, she told him that she'd said all she wanted to say to her family and now she wanted to be comfortable. He agreed to prescribe more sedation and then asked if he could do anything else for her. I'll never forget her reply: "Come often. It helps," Catherine said.

I wish all physicians could hear those simple but important words spoken so calmly by a dying patient. Catherine's physician stayed in a comforting silence; no words were necessary.[2]

---

[2] "Sue L. Frymark, "Come Often, It Helps," *American Journal of Nursing*, Wolters Kluwer Health, June 1990, F776.

5

LIVING WITH CHANGE

It takes a while to get through the initial turmoil of a life-threatening illness. It may have felt like an emotional roller coaster; however, over time, the dips may not be as deep, and you may feel ready for a daily routine again. Most people live a few months or years past the diagnosis. So how can you get back to a somewhat normal life?

Fitzhugh Mullan, MD—physician, and cancer survivor—is thought of as a pioneer in the area of cancer survivorship. He discusses the phases of living with a life-threatening illness in his article "Seasons of Survival." The first is the "Acute Phase" when the diagnosis is new, and a treatment management plan is defined. The second is "Extended," when one realizes that he or she might live awhile. The third phase is "Permanent," which may be described as long term. Except for those who die within days or weeks of the diagnosis, most experience all these phases. Mullan focuses not on the medical-treatment aspect, but the living-with aspect of the experience.[3] A survivor is not just someone who gets cured of a disease for life. It can be a person in remission or striving for it. A survivor is someone who moves past the initial diagnosis and treatment and works to create the best life possible for whatever time he or she has left.

Once you have the symptoms identified and managed, your illness becomes more like a chronic illness. Then you can begin the process of making a new life for yourself. It will be different, but it will be valuable. God can and will bless the experience for you and those who walk with you, giving you and your family memorable times together for months or years.

Staying independent as long as possible is the goal for most people. Maintaining strength is important—not only physical strength but mental as well. Focus on wellness even in the face of illness, and it will have a positive impact on your experience. Wellness programs, offered by many community organizations, can be helpful. They focus on healthy living including diet, exercise, and stopping various unhealthy habits such as smoking and excessive drinking. They often have good ideas including recipes, relaxation techniques, and ideas for sleeping better. Some of these organizations offer support groups with others who are also struggling with a life-threatening illness.

Symptom management

Symptom management is especially important. Uncontrolled symptoms, especially pain, can be exhausting and debilitating. A

---

[3] Fitzhugh Mullan, M.D, "Seasons of Survival: Reflections of a Physician with Cancer," *New England Journal of Medicine*, July 25, 1985, 313: 270–73.

pain-care plan can be devised by the health-care professional with you and/or a caregiver. Depending on the illness, it may also involve medications to manage tremors, improve memory, respiratory treatments, muscular spams, or other effects of the illness or treatment. Keep in close contact with your medical team, not only about how medications are working, but in case new symptoms or side effects have occurred. Those whose stress manifests itself as physical symptoms such as headaches, stomach problems, and sleeping difficulties may find relief in physical activities such as calisthenics, walking, running, or swimming. The medical team can help develop physical exercises, within the confines of the disease, that will help you regain at least some strength and endurance. It also helps lift your mood and gives you confidence. Having a good quality of life means living to the fullest.

Try to keep busy

Keeping busy is different for every person and varies during various phases of the disease. At times you may be too busy with treatments and doctors' appointments. During down times, keep busy by having a plan. Of course, rest needs to be part of your plan. Fill your day, not only with obligations, but with things you enjoy. For some, just reading a book or watching a good movie may be the ticket. Distractions can reduce anxiety and stress, allowing you to decompress for a while. It can be healing, especially when reading God's word and devotionals.

Create personal goals

Keep in mind that people are often not successful because they set unrealistic or unattainable goals. Break them down into short-term achievable goals. For example, you might not be able to walk a mile, but you could handle one block. Add rewards to your goals. If you do not feel confident, consider adjusting your goals in the area of doubt. Including family and friends into your activities adds fun and motivation and creates memories. It is good to focus on something else besides your physical difficulties.

Ideas to maximize your quality of life

This is a new experience you may have never been through before. Lifelong coping skills may not work well anymore. Be open to new ideas and suggestions as these can be helpful. Look at your life now and identify personal areas for improvement. Watch for subtle signs of worry and anxiety. These can show up as an inability to concentrate or memory loss, trouble sleeping, or feeling depressed. Worry makes pain caused by the disease worse—sometimes much worse. Share these feelings with your medical team too because sometimes medications and treatments can cause anxiety or depression.

Ideas to relieve stress and take your mind off physical symptoms include:

- Journaling or writing
- Pray or join a prayer group
- Resume or begin volunteer or club activities
- Internet may provide entertainment during times of physical impairment
- Yoga or other relaxing exercises
- Talking or visiting with friends and family
- Games such as crossword puzzles and word searches
- Stay physically active to maintain muscle strength
- Eat healthy including changes necessary in reducing the risk of medical complications
- Draw closer to your spiritual life and community
- Focus on healing relationships with others
- Identify meaningful activities for you
- Join a small support group, church care group, or Bible study group
- Outdoor activities such as gardening, walking, bird watching, and other outdoor activities
- Pursue hobbies such as woodworking, photography, or family genealogy
- Create a bucket list but be realistic about your capabilities and your finances.

Some people who are diagnosed early in the disease process may stay independent and able to continue working. Work is often important. It can be a part of how we define ourselves: "I am a long-distance truck driver" or "I am a teacher." It is also a major source of income and health insurance benefits. Many employers are supportive and creative in helping employees maximize their benefits and adjust their hours if needed. Federal programs such as FMLA (Family Medical Leave), can help people protect their jobs due to medical absences from work for as long as possible if that is what they want to do.

Caregiving

A caregiver is defined as someone who has concern for the welfare of a person who is ill or living with a chronic illness and is involved with his or her care even at the smallest level. One in four adults are caregivers in some way at some point in their lives. A caregiver is concerned about the physical, emotional, social, and spiritual needs of the person. Caregivers don't necessarily live with the ill person, who may not need constant physical assistance. One person may be the primary caregiver but may involve several others. There may be a paid caregiver to allow family members to work or have a break. The amount of physical caregiving needed may increase or fluctuate over time depending on the disease. It is helpful for caregivers to learn about the specific illness, especially to understand the natural progression and possible complications. Each ill person has a host of individualized factors that affect the disease progression and length of time. Some diseases have remission periods that can be quite long, but others only offer a short break.

Disease-specific organizations offer valuable information about that disease and the caregiving issues. For example, the American Parkinson's Disease Association has information about the development of tremors or rigidity—how this affects daily activities and how caregivers can help. Also check organizations related to caregiving in general.

When more intense in-home care is necessary, multiple caregivers may become involved. It is important to create a check list of specific care needs such as the names of medications and times when they are to be given, questions for the doctors, medical appointments, important phone numbers, and whatever else may be useful. Also, maintain a logbook of when medications or treatments are given, the name of the person giving them, and any reactions that may have occurred. These two documents should be reviewed by all the other caregivers, family members involved, and by the professionals who may visit as part of home health, palliative care, or hospice.

> **Angie's story.** My husband was diagnosed with cystic fibrosis. I was so shocked because I thought we had more time. I remember going to the chapel at the hospital and just losing it. I was crying and upset, and I couldn't let John see I was upset. I was trying to hold it together for everybody. You're worried about your husband, and then you're worried about your child because he's losing his dad. There comes a point where you hit the wall and then, at that point, you must do something for you. This experience has made me grateful for every day.

As the caregiver, it is important to stay as healthy as possible. This means eating healthy, drinking fluids regularly, exercising, and getting enough good sleep. This may seem impossible sometimes.

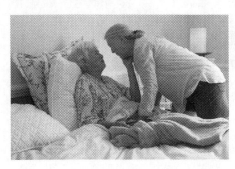 Busy caregivers often neglect themselves. If you are the primary caregiver, the ill-person is dependent on you to do a good job of caregiving. If you don't take care of yourself, you cannot give your loved one the best care possible. Sometimes you may get so busy that you do not recognize your own stress level. Take the comments of others who are concerned about you seriously if they express concerns that you are not taking care of yourself. Family members need to help each other monitor their stress levels and offer to relieve one another as necessary.

Begin by setting some short-term realistic goals. For example, set a reminder to have a glass of water at specific times; take sixty seconds a few times a day to close your eyes and breathe deeply and slowly;

or engage in a hobby such as knitting or drawing. These daily habits help one feel energized and confident.

Caregivers who live with their ill loved ones are particularly vulnerable to stress-related problems. If this is you, you may have a strong sense of loyal obligation. Looking for things that are stressful may go against the grain, as you may have spent years or decades learning to ignore them. But things have changed. There will be impactful situations that can cause stress and cannot be ignored. For example, it can seem like forever for the ill person to take his or her pills, the ill person will not eat beneficial foods, or the person simply will not cooperate with small things like getting dressed. These can be small issues, but over the course of days or weeks, they can take a heavy toll. The ill person can become a fall risk but may not always cooperate with precautions. A change in the mental abilities of the ill person may be among the most difficult changes to handle.

Don't try to be the sole caregiver. There are organizations that offer help. It can be helpful to discuss these issues with the visiting home health, palliative care, or hospice team. They are your consultants. It is important to use the support resources of social workers, nurses, chaplains, family clergy, and the local Christian ministries.

Allow others to help

Family gatherings or meetings are a good time to suggest tasks others may do to help. You might be surprised how willing others can be. Many want to show their support, which can be done by helping. Make a list of one-time or weekly tasks such as mowing the lawn, taking the TV in for repair, or picking up a prescription. These tasks or errands may seem simple but go a long way to reducing stress. Someone who worries he or she cannot help may feel the freedom to do a specific task. Mowing the lawn once a week will be simple for someone.

There may be family members who do not appreciate how

stressed you are or will not help as much as you need them to. They can simply be oblivious to the stress level of a fellow family caregiver. Sometimes they may be experiencing anxiety they don't know how to cope with, or they may feel so much pressure from their life commitments that they do not see how they can help. For these family members, having a list of specific tasks may help them become involved.

As the disease progresses, there may be more and more responsibilities for caregivers. Sadness, loneliness, and anger can signal a mild or serious depression. You may feel drained and exhausted. Your caregiving can overshadow all the rest of daily life. This can be a warning sign. It is important to discuss the care plan with the health-care team to help intervene or monitor the situation before it starts to impact your sleep and eating habits. It is time to revisit the care plan with family and the medical team. Numerous studies have shown that family caregivers have a greater incidence of depression than the general population.

Caregiver support groups are helpful for some, while others find support in a church care group or Bible study. Over time the stress may build. Despite efforts to care for yourself, you may still experience stress. If not dealt with, you may feel overwhelmed and may be unable to continue caregiving. You may begin to feel no one else can provide the care you do and therefore you cannot let go. You might become negative and argumentative, making it difficult for others to help. Some call this burnout. However, you can recover from this exhaustion by taking a break and taking care of yourself. It is important to keep your life in balance. Taking care of yourself means you can better provide for your loved one.

Caregiving is a privilege. It allows us to develop a deeper bond with our loved one. For family caregivers it can be an opportunity to spend time reviewing family experiences and to be reminded of the wonderful memories of times together. There are some who use the time for reconciliation, to heal past wounds and express regret for words exchanged. You are many other things besides a caregiver, including a child of God. He is there to care for you and will comfort you. He will give you the strength, the patience, the comfort, the grace, and the ability to forgive with peace that passes all understanding.

Emily's story. My father was never abusive, but he had high expectations for his children. As a teenager, I felt I could never please him. My parents weren't getting along. I felt my mother's unhappiness as if it were my own. After I left for college, my parents divorced. I was relieved and took their divorce as permission for me to divorce my dad too. I did not see or speak to him for many years.

Thanks to my stepmother, I entered a somewhat distant relationship, and he was able to get to know my children. Then he was diagnosed with stage four lung cancer. In his last days, I would go to help my stepmother care for him—I fed him and helped him

stand up. My bitterness toward him dropped away! Years of feeling unloved and unappreciated miraculously disappeared. My new appreciation for him never went away.

One day, my aunt on my father's side told me something about my dad. His mother was a cold and self-centered person. She died when I was young, so I have few memories of her except that she gave all of us kids a nickel when she would come over for dinner. We were thrilled! When my dad was of preschool age, his mother became angry with him. She then refused to speak to him or care for him for over a year! My aunt, who was only a few years older, fed him, held him when he cried in grief over the rejection of his mother, and stood at the bus stop when my dad started preschool. It's a miracle my dad did not turn out to be a psychopath!

Effects on marriage

There is no doubt that a life-threatening illness has an impact on marriages. Marital relations may change, including the possibility that sex may become difficult, especially if the ill person is fatigued or has other medical issues. The healthy spouse feels out of control and, paradoxically, can feel more loss than the ill person. To safeguard against damage to the marriage, work right from the time of the diagnosis to include the healthy spouse in the process, helping him or her feel empowered. Couples often try to protect each other from difficult information. Although this may be an instinctive reaction, openly sharing information and listening to feelings is critical for the marriage. Couples who can walk through this experience step by step by going to appointments with each other and handling changes together often feel closer than ever before. It brings strength and blessings to both their lives.

A new normal

Your life will change as you walk through the journey of a life-threatening illness. At some point, you may have to create a "new normal" lifestyle. It may not be possible to maintain long-established family traditions. This may cause grief and add to a sense of gloom about the future. Instead, try to maintain family traditions but change the way you participate in them. For example, instead of fixing a meal for everyone, have a potluck; if you can no longer travel, take a trip to your local park. If you are not be able to keep up with your chores around your home, hire someone to do the heaviest, most difficult tasks. Meal preparation may become difficult. Consider having groceries and meals delivered. Meals on Wheels is a nonprofit organization that delivers hot meals to shut-ins at no cost.

Keep in mind that some remodeling of the home, or minor additions recommended by occupational therapists and other experts, can greatly increase your ability to function at home longer and with less stress. For example, replacing a standard bathtub with a walk-in tub can make a big difference. Even if you regain some strength and endurance, these modifications can continue to be beneficial.

Taking control of your daily life will bring back a sense of confidence. You can remain realistic and still be hopeful. Focus on today's reality. Try to be flexible as you go through changes. Recognize your personal strengths and limitations. Learn to ask for help. Become a leader of your own life, not just a follower. Look for meaning and purpose for yourself. Reach out and give of yourself. Serving others gives us a new perspective, takes the focus off ourselves, and gives us a sense of purpose.

The most effective means of coping is to walk closer to Christ day by day through prayer and reading the scriptures. He will be with you through every moment. The disease does not define who you are. It may be a time to explore the question, "Who am I now?" or more importantly, "Who am I in the Father's eyes? How would Jesus describe me?" You are a child of God destined by Him for glory. The Lord will continue to use our lives until He calls us home. Only He knows the time and place. You have a purpose on this earth set by God before your birth. Sink into who God has called you to be. You are still precious to Him.

6

WAITING ON GOD'S TIMING—
VICKI'S STORY

Vicki lived with stage four breast cancer for thirteen years. During that time, she had a strong faith in Christ, which helped her greatly in dealing with treatments, setbacks, and pain.

She and her husband Bob carefully planned for her end of life. She was a well-organized person and used this skill to make things much easier for her loved ones by making sure everything was in order.

She gave her family a great gift. After her death, they were able to take care of her estate with ease. She also blessed her family by creating a scrapbook for each one of them, which included a letter of love and encouragement. Right up to the end, she continued to pray for others.

This testimony came from an interview about six months before her death. Here is her story.

Since I've had cancer, I have been more interested in death because it's been looming right there. You think of it more often. I believe that God is in control, and when He wants me with Him in Heaven and glory, I will be there. Until then I will be here on earth. I kind of wish I knew His timeline a little more because I feel I have an obligation and an urgency to prepare other people around me for what's going to happen to me. I know, well, we all know, we'll be dying, but I have this to think about because it is looming right in front of me quite often. How do you deal with that, and how do you talk about that to your friends? Everybody, not everybody but most people, tend to think that death is the worst thing that can happen. Well, as a believer, that's not true—it's the best thing. That's the end of my road. That's where it all begins again for me. And so, I'm trying to share with people my feelings about this. Not only do I feel the Lord is calling me home soon; He is giving me something to do between now and then—preparation. I'm getting prepared. I pray. I need to be prepared to go to Heaven. I want to be prepared. And I want those around me to be prepared. I know that people will miss me. But I'll see them again. If they're a believer, they'll be in Heaven with me. We'll see each other again. I don't want just this earth to be the most important thing in our lives. I am really Heaven oriented right now. Bob and I have been feeling that this is my calling; I'm not going to be here for a long time. My time is short.

There's a lot that we can do while we're on earth that will make it easier for people after we're gone. I have made a book for each of my two children and my husband. I am trying to contribute to their heritage, showing them what a blessing they have been. But also, in my books, I've put the important things that have happened to me in my spiritual life—when I became a Christian, when I realized that I was serving the Lord, when He called me to certain things. This is documented in my life, and that's important to me. Some of these are things people should do anyway. You should have a record of your possessions. And we should have fewer possessions. That's one of the things we've been doing. We've been trying to simplify my life, so that I am not surrounded by stuff that I don't need or use. A few years ago, I just felt the Lord was leading us to give away a lot of things and especially things we weren't using. If somebody else has a better use for it or would benefit from it, do it, because we've accumulated a lot of things that we don't need. I didn't want someone to have to clean my drawers out! I want to organize it and do it myself. This is my stage for now. I won't have it later.

I like to plan and anticipate events like vacations or birthday parties or whatever. I get a lot of joy from planning these and just looking forward to having a good time. It's interesting because the Bible tells us over and over to remember the Word of God and to teach our children and remember what He has done for us (Psalms 103: 17–18). We even take communion in remembrance of Christ's death and the symbol that He is coming again. That's in Luke 22:19.

I think remembering a person's life is good. For people like me who like to plan, I'm going to plan a lot of my own service because I want people to know who I was and what the Lord meant to me. Whether it be a celebration of life or memorial service or whatever,

I think there's a certain pleasure that can come from preparing and working on your own. Plus, I think it can be a big help and alleviate a lot of stress for your family members. So, write down a few favorite songs or scriptures or maybe the person you want to sing for you or maybe even some food that you like.

I knew a man who wanted to serve peanut butter and honey sandwiches at his memorial service because he had thirteen grandchildren, and it was a special thing between him and all his grandchildren to have these sandwiches. So that's what they had at his service. At the funeral of another friend, they served bowls of popcorn because he loved popcorn so much. You hardly ever went to their house without having popcorn. He'd bring a special kind of popcorn to your house. So just a special connection between me and the people that are left behind and it's a positive thing.

Scriptures are very comforting to me now. One of my favorites is Psalm 121:8: "'The Lord shall preserve thy going out and thy coming in from this time forth, and even for evermore.'" (KJV)

7

PLANNING FOR THE FUTURE

My health may fail, and my spirit may grow weak,
but God remains the strength of my heart; he is mine
forever. (Psalm 73:26 NLT)

We can never predict the exact timeframe of a life-threatening illness. A prognosis is just a guesstimate. People often live longer than expected, but sometimes death comes more quickly than anyone thought. Resolving issues and planning for possible future events will be helpful, not only for you, but your family as well. This is best done while you are feeling well.

Not everyone will be emotionally ready to discuss end-of-life issues and planning. Still, it is important to get started. Although it may seem hard, you will be relieved by taking care of what you can. Common concerns are: Will your spouse or family have access to your financial accounts, bills, will, and insurance plans? What about passwords, keys, and locks, and what about important names with contact information?

Financial plans and wills

Create a financial plan that encompasses the possibility you will need help in this area. Family businesses may need a separate succession plan. Estate attorneys are skilled in end-of-life planning as well as retirement and will make sure your assets are distributed according to your wishes in the most effective manner. If you do not already have a will, you should get one as soon as possible. Wills written close to the time of death are more easily contested. Be sure to designate the executor.

You should create plans for other important issues like who will take your pets and how will their needs be paid for. For single parents of young children at home, a financial plan is critical. Someone may agree to adopt the children, but is it official, and how will this be paid for? Be sure to contact an expert in child-custody issues.

Obtain information, including costs, about potential resources such as transportation services, housekeeping, companion care, or aging-in-place remodelers. Begin to explore the costs of funerals and alternative living situations. Consider setting up a joint bank account so that someone else can pay the regular bills and access funds immediately after death.

If you have a long-term care policy, review it to understand what and when coverage can start. Look for other policies you may have, such as life, disability, and funeral policies and make sure you understand their benefits and restrictions.

You may be reluctant, but it is highly advisable that you share your finances with your family. Unfortunately, serious splits over money happen quite often. If you don't want to reveal dollar amounts, at least share the general plan such as what percent will go to which successors, or which properties you want sold rather than distributed. Depending on the size of your estate, your loved ones could end up in court for years.

Consider giving away some things early. These are items that would probably not be listed in a will. Family members often treasure small inexpensive things. Your cup collection or your special flowers may have no monetary value but be important to others.

Important documents to consider

Identify or obtain important documents that will be needed for planning or for family in settling final affairs. If possible, keep them in a binder or file. Consider storing them in a place where others can find them. Be sure that passwords, keys, and lock combinations are available. Have lists of names and numbers of advisers, doctors, attorneys, and insurance companies. These documents may include:

- Will and/or living trust and the location of these
- Name of attorney or location of will
- Advance Directive indicating your medical preferences for treatment/care
- POLST (Provider Orders for Life-Sustaining Treatment) form to be kept in a visible place in case of urgent medical problems
- Power of attorney for health care
- Naturalization papers
- Birth certificate and Social Security card
- Marriage and/or divorce certificates
- Military papers
- Insurance papers including life and disability

- Income tax records
- Financial papers related to stocks, bonds, annuities
- Prepaid funeral services
- Long-term-care policies or funds
- Property ownership papers (i.e., automobiles, vacation homes, time-shares)

Be prepared for in-home care

You never know if you will need in-home support or not. Planning in advance helps avoid quick decisions that might not work out well. It makes living easier, both for you and the family caregivers, if the disease progresses and disabilities increase. Some physical issues are difficult for the caregiver to handle without help. Rearranging or remodeling the home may allow the person to stay at home longer. Risks for falling and injury need to be addressed. A physical therapist and/or an occupational therapist can assess this and make recommendations as well as instruct the family in safety. They may suggest assistive devices such as walkers, raised toilet seats, or special eating utensils that will make daily life easier and safer. There are companies and organization that work to help people remain in the home as long as possible by making modifications as needs change. Don't be afraid to change agencies if you are unhappy with care or cannot communicate with them. A nurse or social worker involved in the care can be your advocate.

Here is a list of types of organizations and professionals that might be helpful:

- Private home care services
- Aging & Disability Services
- Meals on Wheels
- Palliative and hospice care

- Agencies that provide housekeeping, child-care, dog walkers, gardeners, etc.
- Senior centers and community aging and disability agencies
- Social worker with healthcare provider (i.e., hospital or hospice)
- Case manager with the health insurance company
- "It's about how you live," http://www.caringinfo.org.

Many states have websites for aging and people with disabilities offering important resources for public assistance whether medical care, caregiving support, or food assistance.

Critical medical decisions

Making end of life choices for yourself or your loved one may be the most difficult decision you will ever have to make. This is why it is so important that you know what you want *before* the time comes when you are in a medical crisis and the doctor is asking you what you want to do. Be sure you have good and accurate medical information. If possible, discuss options in a family meeting that includes someone from the medical team. Even though the decision is yours, your loved ones will benefit greatly by having the opportunity to share their feelings. It is one of the most thoughtful gifts you can leave for your family and friends, so they don't have to guess what you want when they are in a very emotional state. The Advance Directive is the primary method for communicating these choices. It is helpful to carry a short medical summary of diagnosis, medical issues, and medications in case of an emergency.

Advance Care Directive

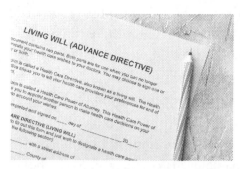

The Advance Care Directive is a form that outlines medical treatments you want or don't want at the end of your life. Typically, it asks if you want to refuse the use of feeding tubes, ventilators, or CPR, (cardiopulmonary resuscitation.) Some ask the same questions under different circumstances such as, "Is death expected to be imminent due to the disease?" or "Is the treatment expected to prolong life and improve quality of life?" Related questions may piggyback on the form, such as "Do you want to be an organ donor?" It identifies who you want to speak on your behalf if you become mentally or physically unable to make decisions for yourself. This person is usually called the "Durable Power of Attorney for Healthcare," or your "Health Care Proxy." Samples are available from a variety of sources, including hospice websites, Aging and Disability Services website, AARP, doctors' offices, and hospitals.

It is important to inform your physician of your end-of-life wishes and the person who will be your designated representative. Also, share your end-of-life wishes with your family. This not only improves your chances that your wishes will be respected, it also helps your loved ones avoid arguing about end-of-life decisions.

Over time, your wishes may change, so review it from time to time. Feel free to modify your Advance Directive any time but make sure your family and medical team know about it.

POLST

The POLST form (Physician Orders for Life-Sustaining Treatment) is an official document that the physician signs. It becomes part of the medical record and is registered in a statewide database. At home, keep it in a visible place in case of emergency. Without it, first responders may not listen to verbal requests. The POLST form ensures your wishes are respected.

Even though others give input, the decisions belong primarily to the ill person if he or she is capable of making decisions. If the ill person is not able to make decisions, every effort should be made to reflect what the ill person would most likely choose.

One family was told by an emergency physician that they had five minutes to decide if their mother should be put on a respirator. Anxiety quickly set in until they realized their mother had already made that decision, and she did not want that intervention. They had no regrets and were able to stay at her side thanking her for being a wonderful mother and lifting her up in prayer. One son noted "she looks beautiful, look at her face. All the stress of the world is gone." She not only died in peace, but her family experienced the same peace even in their sorrow.

Palliative care

Palliative care is a holistic approach to improve symptom management while also addressing emotional and spiritual aspects of the experience. Programs use a team approach to bring multifaceted skills to support, educate, and problem-solve care issues with the family. Often physicians from differing disciplines are included. Some insurance programs define this as having a prognosis of two years. Some chronic illness, such as congestive heart or kidney failure, Alzheimer's, and Parkinson's disease, that have an uncertain prognosis from the perspective of time frame, may still be covered by the program. Medical treatments can continue to be curative, but comfort and quality of life become the major emphasis. If, at some point, symptoms become more severe resulting in more calls to the doctor or trips to the emergency room, it may be time to consider palliative care.

Hospice

Hospice is defined, primarily by insurance companies, as having a prognosis of six months or less. Like palliative care, Hospice uses a team approach that includes social workers, physical, occupational, and speech therapists, chaplains, and trained volunteers. The decision to go onto hospice services can be difficult. It requires the individual and the doctor to agree in writing with the prognosis. Some people have a hard time letting go of curative treatments even when they are no longer helpful and could be considered futile. Pain, symptom management, quality of life, and staying at home for as long as possible are the primary goals of hospice.

In-home hospice care requires a family member to be the primary caregiver. The team will make regular visits to assess needs and problem solve with the family and caregivers. Hospice teams can be helpful in making care easier in the home and help family understand any changes that may be occurring. Some additional care may be needed with bathing and personal care, that the hospice team can help arrange. A hospice nurse is available twenty-four hours a day. This can be a huge comfort to families who may worry that new problems might arise.

Trained volunteers are available for respite care allowing the family caregiver to have a break or time for errands. Spiritual care counselors (chaplains) are also part of the team. However, they are not all Christian. They do not take the place of pastors from a church. Social workers can also help with end-of-life planning and with communicating those wishes with the family. They can also work to help reconcile family relationships. The social worker and the nurses can help with family meetings. The hospice team members become an important part of the family's support network and can help carry out final wishes if requested.

Rehabilitation disciplines help families adapt the home or remodel certain areas to help the ill person live at home longer and make care more manageable. Remodeling the bathroom to accommodate a walker or wheelchair, for example, might be all that is needed to help the ill person to stay at home. Occupational therapists are particularly helpful in suggesting low-cost ideas to make care at home more manageable. This is important for family caregivers in preventing stress and burnout.

At times they may stay in a nursing care facility or the hospital temporarily. Hospice doctors and nurses who are experts in end-of-life care oversee care in these settings as well.

People can, and do, move off hospice because they stabilize, their prognosis changes, or because they decide to pursue curative treatments. Sometimes they improve after problematic symptoms have been addressed. Then they can return to hospice if the prognosis changes back to six months or less.

Out of home care

It may become necessary to consider the possibility of placement outside the home. The medical or mental condition of the ill person may progress to the point where the caregivers can no longer keep the ill person safe and medically managed. Types of facilities include:

- Skilled nursing (highly regulated)
- Intermediate care
- Adult living including assisted living
- Adult care homes (adult foster care) have fewer regulations
- Memory care facilities

- Day care facilities
- Respite care facilities
- Hospice in-patient facilities
- Assisted living where spouse or caregiver and ill person live together
- Retirement communities of homes, condominiums, and apartments. These often have graduated levels of care available.

Planning the memorial service

Planning your own memorial or celebration of life spares your family from having to do this after you are gone when they will be grieving or feel overwhelmed by other issues. Funeral homes usually have booklets to guide you through the process. Putting your own service together will better reflect who you are through photo displays, songs chosen, reflection of your faith, and type of reception, if desired. Planning involves working with a funeral home, crematorium, or church and clergy for those of faith. The ideal is for the family to participate. For some, it is too emotional, but some will enjoy organizing photos, life story displays, and videos. For many, viewing photos brings back positive memories and helps with the grieving process. Most say they are relieved by having it done even if it is not needed for a few years. It has been described as a great gift to the family, who are then free to grieve during the last days. It can leave a positive imprint on the family.

The Bible does not dictate that a certain burial method must be used. The tradition of the Hebrews was to bury the dead, but this may have been to distinguish themselves from pagan cultures. Saul and Jonathan were cremated (1 Samuel 31:12). God does not need our bodies to be intact. He will raise our remains, regardless of their condition, and make them into imperishable eternal bodies. "In the same way, our earthly bodies which die and decay are different from the bodies we shall have when we come back to life again, for they will never die" (1 Corinthians 15: 42 TLB). The decision to cremate or not is basically personal, cultural, or denominational. One person who took our class shared that her young children were horrified that their father, who had just passed away, might feel being burned if cremation was used, so burial was selected.

Taking inventory

This is a time to look back on your life and decide which events were the most important to you. Who did you love? Which decisions changed your life? These aspects of our lives shape the legacy we leave behind in the memories of others. A spiritual inventory means being honest about our relationship with God—with Jesus Christ. Have we been honest with Him about our shortcomings, about those things in our lives we feel guilty about? What is on your mind that weighs you down? Are these thoughts making you fear God? We need not be fearful for He is a loving God who already knows us but is simply waiting for us to lay those thoughts and fears at his feet. We will be forgiven, and this grace is a gift. It is a freedom that allows us to live with joy no matter what the circumstances.

> If we confess our sins, he is faithful and just to forgive
> us our sins, and to cleanse us from all unrighteousness.
> (1 John 1:9 KJV)

You may need to reach out to someone to bring that person back into your life. If you need to, apologize to someone or forgive someone. However, there may have been people from your past who are not safe. Maybe there was drug or alcohol abuse, poverty, domestic violence, or child abuse. These factors may have led to divorce. It may not be a good idea to reach out to every person who hurt you. However, there may be a wound in your heart that could use healing. Think about seeking help from a professional counselor or pastor. Forgiving those who hurt us will set us free. Putting those issues to rest will help you get more out of the relationships you have now.

How we love, forgive, and appreciate those around us impacts how we prepare for the end of life. We have seen families reunite after years and often remain together during those last hours of their loved one's life. We have seen divorced spouses become caregivers to their former spouse. Lift the situation up in prayer. Because He first loved us, we can love others. Nothing is impossible with the Lord.

Leaving a legacy

As you plan for the future, you may find yourself looking back on your life. These memories are part of your legacy. Share them with your family. Help them understand who the Lord is to you and how He has affected your life. Give them the gift of putting your life into writing so they will not forget. Ideas for doing this include:

- Write letters to your loved ones.
- Gather and catalog photos and other memorabilia.
- Write out stories about different family members.
- Share genealogy findings as part of the family history.
- Releasing your loved ones by encouraging them to heal and move on with their future.
- Spouses may think about the concept of a future remarriage.
- Journal about your experience.

Help and reassure children who may fear being alone and unprotected. Providing them a loving and supportive environment over the course of the illness is the best way to reduce anxieties.

Family members can demonstrate their love and grace to reassure the ill person, who may feel he or she is abandoning the family.

Your legacy will bless your loved ones for generations. God created this phenomenon to strengthen society. Families will feel grief and loss. God will take care of your loved one when you are gone. God will use this experience beyond your expectations.

> Father to the fatherless, defender of the widows—this is God whose dwelling is holy. (Psalm 68:5 NLT)

8

THROUGH THE EYES OF A
CHILD—RACHEL'S STORY

 I would say that my
journey begins all the
way back when I was
two years old. My
mother was diagnosed
with myasthenia gravis, which is a neuro-muscular
disease that basically affects the muscle's ability to
respond and be strong, which included anything from
speech to swallowing to walking—anything that had
to do with her muscles. So, I became the second mom
of the home because, when Mom would go across the
street to get the mail, it would be so much wear and
tear on her body that she would then be in bed for
three days. She would have to sit on the couch or in
a reclining chair to eat. We didn't have many family
dinners when I was young.

As a young girl I did not understand, so many times trips to the hospital meant there were tantrums. I feared visiting the hospital. It was not a place where I wanted to be. I didn't even recognize my mom there. I didn't want to go into the room. So, for them, it was easier if I just stayed with grandparents or childcare.

Then my mom went through some tough physical battles. At that point, she was close to dying. I remember my mom praying, "God I will minister to my family if you get me through." And that's exactly what my mom has done for the last twenty-six years. But I have to tell you that when you're young, you don't understand. All I understood was that mom was sick and that she needed my help. So that's the role that I took on—I was mamma's little helper and even a second mom to my brother.

You know, there are times God just blesses you with funny moments. And as a family you look back and just kind of laugh. There was an afternoon when my mom had been on high doses of Prednisone. My dad and I sat on the couch and watched my mom bake thirteen apple pies in one afternoon because the Prednisone was just roaring through her body. You just think back, and as ugly as Prednisone was, it was the thing that probably helped her most in the moment.

As a believer, all you want is for God to come, and you want God to heal, and you want God to take it. And you forget that sometimes God heals, and God takes things and uses other things beyond just a full healing. And there did come a night when I was about 10—we were sitting in the living room eating. My brother and I got special permission to eat on TV trays that night. Then my mom started choking. We knew to stay calm. We knew to watch and listen, and if there was no air coming out, then that was our cue. If she wasn't making any noise, we needed to take it a step further. And I remember peeking my head around into the kitchen as my mom was leaning over the sink, trying to breathe. And my heart pounded. All I could do for her was to lay my little hand on her back and say "Jesus, make her breath." At that moment she breathed! Something inside of me at that moment knew that God cared. So small, but God cared.

We must have stood beside my mom twice a month to pray for healing. It didn't seem to come. And so you begin to doubt if it's even possible or if God even cares in that way. But I learned at a young age that healing looks different to God. And He began to place that healing touch in my eyes to remind me that He was there. And that was enough to get me through and to remind me that he cared for me and he cared for my mom.

There came a time when both my brother and I got chicken pox. The doctor was going to have to remove my mom from the home because if she got chicken pox, it would put her in the hospital—any large illness, her immune system would not be able to handle it. And it ended up she got tested, and she was immune from chicken pox! Never have I ever heard of anyone being immune, but that was another thing that God used to show He cared—so small, but God cared.

As time went on, I got extremely sick my junior year of high school. I had mono. And then again, because of my brother's age and my age, I was going to stay with my grandparents because of my mom's illness. She was still in a weak state. Most people couldn't tell she had this disease, except that her voice was soft or she wouldn't have a ton of energy. She still tried to stay involved and take us kids on field trips. But if she did that, the next day she would do nothing. It was kind of, you give all one day and take two days to recover. The pastor came up to my house to visit us before I was going to have to leave, and he prayed for me. The next day I woke up completely healed. I had mono for two days—two and a half! For that is just another way that showed God cared.

You know, in the back of your mind, you always wonder "Is it possible?" I don't think that I ever stopped believing that it could happen; I just got used to what my mom had. We never stopped praying, but the frequency of our prayers was less—mom didn't go up to the altar every time to pray for healing. You just kind of got used to it. But you always hoped. And I think it says that He who started a good work in you will be faithful to complete it. I think I always had the picture of what that completion would look like. But God had a different picture of what completion looked like. It was still healing, but it hasn't come around in full. To this day my mom is not 100 percent healed, but she has been healed in other ways and been able to do certain things that she shouldn't have been able to do. She shouldn't have been able to come out of surgery; she shouldn't have been able to take kick-boxing classes or ride a bike around a lake; she shouldn't have been able to play with her granddaughter on the floor. But she did, and those little things are healing.

Now that I'm twenty-eight years old and married and have a little girl, I'm just amazed at the faithfulness—that God had protected my parents' marriage, that my brother and I are both strong in our relationship with the Lord, and that my mom got to watch us grow up. Those little things are healing. It hasn't come around in full, but we believe that her eternal healing is when she meets Jesus face to face. I don't think she is going to ask, "Why didn't you?" I think she'll just say, "Thank you."

As difficult as it can be, and there're some days I wish I could just drive down and help her out, because she's having a tough day, or mentally she's worn down. I just think, *God, you still care. You have never left us nor forsaken us. You didn't give us this to teach us a lesson. Yes, you have used us to teach us many lessons and for my mom spiritually to grow, but that's the healing. And that's the faithfulness.* We would 100 percent love our mom to be cured, but it's God's faith, and compassion and provision and eternal love for us outstretches her healing.

That's the kind of family we are today. We keep walking, and we keep praying, and we're thankful that we had our mom twenty-six years longer than we should have. And if we get to have her one more day, then that's the blessing. And that's my story.

9

DEALING WITH THE WHY

Asking God "why" might be saddest question we will ever ask. As we sit beside the bed of a dying loved one, how do we cope with his or her suffering? We cry out, "Why me?" "Why my loved one?" "Why my innocent child?" This is a cry that comes from our souls. How can a loving God allow so much suffering to go on in the world?

We all hope we can die pain free, in our sleep, at an old age after a full life. But what happens when the dying person is a child or a single parent? What if he or she is suffering great pain or lost in dementia? If you are the ill person, you may fear the progression of the disease, or wonder how your family will cope without you, especially if they are dependent on you. How can God let this happen? Why does the dying process have to be so difficult?

It is natural to ask why. And it is natural to feel it is just not fair. Even if your faith is strong, you may question your own beliefs. Is God really good? Did I do something wrong? Does He care about what happens to me? When we are suddenly forced to deal with a life-threatening illness, erroneous thinking about God is common because we are trying to find an answer we can understand. The struggle to explain the problem of suffering is as old as religion itself.

Punishing

Sometimes people feel that God is a judgmental punishing God. Does He use sickness to punish us? Does he give a long life only to people who really deserve it? If this were true, God would punish all the worst people and only the good ones would be left. If we look at our violent world today, we know this cannot be true. Innocent people still suffer. Little children will still be abused and neglected every day. Children of all ages get cancer and die. William Sloane Coffin said, "Almost every square inch of the earth's surface is soaked with the tears and blood of the innocents."[4]

> **The Clara Story.** We had a woman take our Wilderness Journey Ministries classes. Her name was Clara. She was in her eighties and had an aggressive form of lung cancer. She only had a few months to live. When she first came to the class with her daughter, you could tell—she did *not* want to be there. She was dragged there. But after just a few minutes of the class, her whole demeanor began to change. She began to relax and even smile. Toward the end she

---

[4] Langford, James R., and Leroy S. Rouner, *Walking with God in a Fragile World* (Lanham, MD: Rowman & Littlefield, 2003).

said, "This is really nice. I'm going to come back." It was fun to watch her change over the weeks. During one of the classes, we shared that we have a God who is loving and forgiving. Clara shared with us that she had been raised in a church that described God as being judgmental and punishing, and she became afraid of God. After she became a young adult, she decided not to go back to church for that reason. She did not want to be reminded of that kind of God. All those years, she had not been in a church until she came to our class. She was so relieved that God is forgiving and that He loves her. This just radiated in her heart for the rest of the weeks. She became fun to have in the class. In the last class, we always ask everyone what they got out of the classes. Clara answered, "I learned that I don't have to be afraid." That was such a blessing for us.

The next few months were the last months for Clara, but they were good months. She spent time with some important people in her life. When she died, her family surrounded her including an ex-husband who had reconciled with the family. It was really a beautiful time for them. Later, her daughter shared with us that all her adult life, she did not have a good relationship with her. After taking our class together, they became close and could talk about so much. She was just grateful for the gift of those last few months. Clara stayed in her home until the last two weeks, when she stayed with her daughter. She died very peacefully.

What does the Bible say about suffering?

The book of Genesis tells us that suffering is a result of man's fall from grace in the Garden of Eden.

> The LORD God placed the man in the Garden of
> Eden to tend and watch over it. But the LORD God
> warned him, "You may freely eat the fruit of every
> tree in the garden—except the tree of the knowledge
> of good and evil. If you eat its fruit, you are sure to
> die." (Genesis 2:15–17 NLT)

Mankind had free run of paradise on earth with only one rule—don't touch the tree of knowledge of good and evil! Remember that Satan, in the form of a snake, suggested the idea that they eat from the tree.

> "Of course, we may eat fruit from the trees in the
> garden," the woman replied. "It's only the fruit from
> the tree in the middle of the garden that we are not
> allowed to eat. God said, 'You must not eat it or even
> touch it; if you do, you will die.'"

> "You won't die!" the serpent replied to the woman.
> "God knows that your eyes will be opened as soon as
> you eat it, and you will be like God, knowing both
> good and evil." (Genesis 3:2–5 NLT)

Satan accused God of not being good. He painted God as selfish, wanting to keep the best for Himself. Adam and Eve fell for the lie. Toil, pain, frustration, and death resulted from their choice. They did not gain what they thought they would gain. But they did gain two things they did not have before—sin and death. And with it came suffering for all humankind.

So, the LORD God banished them from the Garden of Eden, and he sent Adam out to cultivate the ground from which he had been made. (Genesis 3:23–24 NLT)

There is a definite connection between suffering and evil. In fact, suffering is the outcome of the intent of evil to kill and destroy. Adam and Eve could no longer live in the garden of paradise because they were no longer innocent.

Job

The Lord knew that suffering would be one of man's chief stumbling blocks to faith. The book of Job reveals a variety of principles about suffering, given by God, for millions upon millions of people over thousands of years. The first one is that bad things do happen to good people. Job's friends believed that all hardship happened as a result of sin and tried to get him to admit it. God later rebukes them for this. Another principle is that God is always in charge. How can this be? We want God to be all-powerful, so he can heal and protect us. But on the other side of the coin, we don't want Him to be too powerful because we want Him to be loving and kind. How can He be both and allow the Satan/serpent to do so much harm?

Satan's accusation of humankind is that they will only pretend to love God for what they can get out of Him. In hard times, humans will curse God. God offers Satan a challenge that Job will remain faithful.

One day the members of the heavenly court came to present themselves before the LORD, and the Accuser, Satan, came with them. "Where have you come from?" the LORD asked Satan. Satan answered the LORD, "I have been patrolling the earth, watching everything that's going on." Then the LORD asked Satan, "Have you noticed my servant Job? He is the finest man in all the earth. He is blameless—a man of complete integrity. He fears God and stays away from evil." Satan replied to the LORD, "Yes, but Job has good reason to fear God. You have always put a wall of protection around him and his home and his property. You have made him prosper in everything he does. Look how rich he is! But reach out and take away everything he has, and he will surely curse you to your face!" (Job 1:6–11 NLT)

Satan takes everything from Job except his wife and his life. He takes his ten children, his wealth, and his health. Job's response is, of course, profound grief and confusion about God.

Job stood up and tore his robe in grief. Then he shaved his head and fell to the ground to worship. He said, "I came naked from my mother's womb, and I will be naked when I leave. The LORD gave me what I had, and the LORD has taken it away. Praise the name of the LORD!" In all of this, Job did not sin by blaming God. (Job 1:20–22 NLT)

Job cries out to God,

"I cannot keep from speaking. I must express my anguish. My bitter soul must complain. Am I a sea monster or a dragon that you must place me under guard? I think, 'My bed will comfort me, and sleep will ease my misery,' but then you shatter me with dreams and terrify me with visions. I would rather be strangled—rather die than suffer like this. I hate

my life and don't want to go on living. Oh, leave me
alone for my few remaining days." (Job 7:11–16 NLT)

Job's questions for God were much like ours today. Lord, how
could you let this happen? What did I do to deserve this? Just let
me die instead of making me go through this. Job asks why, but he
does not get a direct answer. The creation of the earth was an event
so enormous and complex that no human being can even begin to
understand it. C.S. Lewis says it well when he says, "When I lay these
questions before God, I get no answer. But a rather special sort of 'No
answer.' ... like, 'Peace, child; you don't understand.'"[5]

The story of Job is a story of the testing of the faith of humans
in the face of suffering and of one man who continued to seek God
despite everything. It is a model for all of us. God has a plan for
humankind that spans through the fabric of time and space.

Peter reveals that faith, despite suffering, has eternal purposes.

> All praise to God, the Father of our Lord Jesus Christ.
> It is by his great mercy that we have been born again,
> because God raised Jesus Christ from the dead. Now
> we live with great expectation, and we have a priceless
> inheritance—an inheritance that is kept in Heaven for
> you, pure and undefiled, beyond the reach of change
> and decay. And through your faith, God is protecting
> you by his power until you receive this salvation,
> which is ready to be revealed on the last day for all to
> see. So be truly glad. There is wonderful joy ahead,
> even though you must endure many trials for a little
> while. These trials will show that your faith is genuine.
> It is being tested as fire tests and purifies gold—though
> your faith is far more precious than mere gold. So,
> when your faith remains strong through many trials,

---

[5] C. S. Lewis, <u>A Grief Observed</u> ([San Francisco]: Harper San Francisco, 2001)

it will bring you much praise and glory and honor on the day when Jesus Christ is revealed to the whole world. You love him even though you have never seen him. Though you do not see him now, you trust him; and you rejoice with a glorious, inexpressible joy. The reward for trusting him will be the salvation of your souls. (1 Peter 1:3–9 NLT)

The cross is proof that God really does love us. He sacrificed his Son to save us, not only from original sin, but from the sins we commit every day. It is because Christ suffered that we can trust Him to understand the feelings we experience when we are dealing with a life-threating illness or death. He felt agony, humiliation, fear, and depression, just like us, but without sin. Christ's experience was

meant to be an example of how we are to handle suffering. You have a unique opportunity to glorify God by the way you live with a life-threatening illness. Every aspect of your walk with God shows glory to Him—when you pray, when you trust Him, yes, even when you cry out to Him. God is a healer—He wants to make you whole. Even if a healed body here on earth is not part of His plan for you, He will heal in many other ways. Satan continues to try to separate us from the love of God, but because of the resurrection, the battle has been won!

There comes a time when we must admit that we just can't fix it! This is a humbling experience. We are all going to suffer, and we are all going to die on this earth. But Christianity offers hope that is beyond this earth—that of eternal life with Him in paradise where there is no more pain, no more tears. In the meantime, our loving God promises to be with us as we journey through life and death. God wants us to rely on Him despite the suffering.

You can go to God with your grief questions and even your anger. He will understand. He watched His own Son die too. There isn't any experience on earth He will not understand. He loves you with a love beyond human understanding. His desire is for you to grasp even the smallest kernel of that love. His is a love that transforms.

When your despair is at its greatest, remember to praise God for his goodness. In our human selves, this may be impossible. But in seeking Jesus, we will be imparted with peace. Praising Him will literally decrease your pain and your fear.

Remember God's attributes. He is:

- Merciful
- Faithful
- Always good
- Always perfect
- All knowing
- All powerful
- Always loving

God promises to be with us through our trials. He understands your feelings. In the Beatitudes it says, "Blessed are those who mourn, for they will be comforted" (Matthew 5:4 NLT). God has a soft spot in his heart for you. Jesus suffered great pain and humiliation and died from His wounds. Jesus can really say he knows what we are going through. He will never leave you or forsake you.

> "How great is the love the Father has lavished on us, that we should be called children of God!" (1 John 3:1a NIV).

This time you are experiencing now is temporary. We need to remember that we belong to Him. When we have a heavenly outlook on life, it can change our perception of our current experiences. Problems do not seem quite as dark when we have our eyes on the bright horizon of God's Paradise. After all, for those who know Christ, our deaths are simply the shedding of our earthly vessels. Eternity with Him is The Big Promise. God has a master plan that includes us. No matter what happens in the last stages of life, *God still loves you!* He sees through all sicknesses, disabilities, and conditions to see your heart and soul that He created. He loves you through all stages of living and dying. His plan for you is not wiped out by illness. You do not lose your value and worth because you become sick or incapacitated.

The Weaver

My Life is but a weaving
Between my Lord and me;
I cannot choose the colors
He worketh steadily.
Oft times He weaveth sorrow
And I, in foolish pride,
Forget He sees the upper, and I the underside.
Not till the loom is silent and the shuttles cease to fly,
Shall God unroll the canvas
And explain the reason why.
The dark threads are as needful
In the Weaver's skillful hand,
As the threads of gold and silver
In the pattern He has planned.
He knows, He loves, He cares,
Nothing this truth can dim.
He gives His very best to those
who leave the choice with Him.[6]

---

[6] "The Weaver," by Grant Colfax Tullar, sometimes known as "The Tapestry." Made popular by Corrie ten Boom and John and Elizabeth Sherrill in *The Hiding Place*, Bantam Books, the Netherlands, October 1974.

10

A TESTIMONY OF MY
JOURNEY—SUE'S STORY

After several years of chronic bronchitis and several episodes of pneumonia, my doctor referred me to a lung specialist. As part of a routine workup I had a CAT scan of my respiratory system. I came home to numerous urgent messages. I was sent to the emergency room for fear of a respiratory arrest. I was not concerned yet as I didn't have any trouble breathing. I was watched through the night and had further testing in the morning. I was diagnosed with a rare lung condition—tracheobronchomalecia— where my trachea (windpipe) had become extremely narrow. The cartilage that supports the trachea was gone, allowing it to "flop around." The physicians had a difficult time grasping how I was still alive. In retrospect, we are sure this had been coming on for years. I was stunned by how serious the problem was.

I was told pneumonia would most likely be the cause of my death. I felt like the rug was pulled out from underneath me. I started to cry. He gave me a few moments and then pledged that he would continue to see me through this time. I left his office praying for God's protection and help and wisdom for the physicians.

I went home to tell my siblings and others. Each time I told it, the diagnosis became more real and more frightening. It was naturally upsetting to everyone. I could tell they each needed time to absorb it. I called my pastor, who I knew well as I was very involved in my congregation. I will never forget his response: "I will walk you through it." It was a reminder that Christ would as well.

I feared being alone to cope with this on my own. However, once my family adjusted to the news, they each found their way to help me. My younger brother who had lived with me for some time, continued to care for my home. Over the past year he became my caregiver. He was my medical advocate. He took me to the hospital several times and stayed close. At home he made sure I was comfortable. My sister-in-law became what I called "Mom" always making sure I was taking care of myself and doing what I could to prevent infections. She supplied me with vitamins and sanitizers. My sister, who lived thirty miles away, would come in to help me keep up my home and just visit. Time became precious. The situation went from being "I" centered to "we." They went to my appointments and helped me through making decisions. I was grateful how they each stepped up because I never was good at asking for help.

Being single, I became overwhelmed with putting things in order, which included a home filled with "stuff." For some time, I lived with a sense of urgency. As a result, I made some decisions too quickly, not thinking them through enough. This only led to the need to make some corrections. Fortunately, one of my brothers intervened and from that day forward helped me with some of the legal and financial issues.

After over six months of being treated for lung and sinus tract infections, I wondered when new infections would arise. I spoke with my pastor about a "healing service" that we have from time to time. Friends and past coworkers saw it as an opportunity to have a reunion with many I had not seen for years. Following the service, we had a reception. It was a reminder of how I have been blessed by so many of these men and women. Friends and family came forward to join the prayer and laying on of hands. I was overwhelmed with tears as the Lord so powerfully touched me. After so many months of stubborn infections, I was weary. I now felt renewed and, more importantly, ready to wait upon the Lord. I would stop asking, "How long?" My family frequently would say it is up to God as to when. The urgency was fading.

Over time I could not tolerate much walking or activities. This was frustrating for me. I could not shop in large stores or do much activity such as housework without getting short of breath. I finally agreed to use the scooters in stores and/or a wheelchair. I learned it made me feel more independent. Fortunately, I found many things I could do sitting, especially on the computer, such as shopping, gift buying, and doing organization projects for my church and Wilderness Journey Ministries. Each day has been different, but I am content.

A friend gave me a devotional book that focused on becoming closer to Christ each day; that through His presence we would have hope. I learned to take it day by day by looking to Jesus, the author and perfecter of my faith. As I learned not to let worries roam through my thoughts, I became free. With freedom from worry I could really enjoy those around me and find a joy that only can come with such freeing of the Spirit. I no longer focus on the surety of dying but rather on living and the blessing that brings. Praise the Lord!

Sue Frymark, a child of God the Father.

Let us fix our eyes on Jesus, the author and perfecter of our faith. (Hebrews 12:2)

11

DIFFICULT DECISIONS

You saw me before I was born. Every day of my life was recorded in your book. Every moment was laid out before a single day had passed. How precious are your thoughts about me, O God! They are innumerable! (Psalm 139:16–17 NLT)

Hopefully, you have already had discussions with your doctor and family about your decisions, but, for everyone's sake, it is important to review them again. Now, later in your journey, your viewpoints may have changed. Because these choices are emotionally charged, conflicts can have long-lasting effects on everyone who cares for you. These are your decision to make but making sure everyone knows about them is very important to your loved ones and will be a great gift to them.

Hospice

You may be wondering if it is time to consider hospice. It's common for this decision to be delayed until the last few weeks or days before death. For some, the word *hospice* can mean "actively dying" or "giving up." If you are faced with this decision, you may feel profound grief at first. It feels like "this is it." Although hospice does require changing from a curative plan to a comfort plan, curative types of treatments are available if they can be helpful to the ill person. For example, radiation therapy might be used to reduce pain for certain types of cancers. Antibiotics might be prescribed for a secondary problem, such as a sinus infection. Remember, people can be moved off hospice if a curative procedure looks like it may give the ill person more time. Then they can be moved back on if it comes to that. Because hospice programs offer teams of experts to address many different problems, it may be best to choose it as early as possible if the doctor recommends it.

People who have worked closely with their medical team and have the active support of their loved ones are more likely to choose hospice, not only because they have more information but because they have more trust. We are all afraid of losing control of our bodies. It's instinctual. But if we believe we will be well cared for, the decision is easier. This is one of those times when Christ promises to be with us. Most people know about the beautiful poem "Footprints in the Sand" where the Lord carries us through the most difficult times. This is truth! We can count on Him.

> And you saw how the LORD your God cared for you all along the way as you traveled through the wilderness, just as a father cares for his child. Now he has brought you to this place. (Deuteronomy 1:31 NLT)

Out-of-home care

We suggest you never make a promise about not being placed in a nursing home. You might have to break that promise. It might not be possible to maintain in-home care. The time to consider another care setting is when medical issues or physical care becomes too demanding. The caregiver may need to be employed outside the home or not be able to afford care for a loved one without his or her job. The ill person may become a fall risk, and the caregiver is not able to assist. The person may become disoriented and be up at night, making it impossible for the caregiver to get enough sleep. Sometimes the ill person needs a more secure setting in order to stay safe.

You may feel you are betraying your loved one, especially if there was an agreement to keep the person at home. Moving the ill person does not mean abandoning him or her. Most care centers have flexible visiting hours. Unless the facility is far away, you should be able to visit as often as you want. Some families have a schedule, taking turns visiting. This helps the ill person feel less lonely. Family members such as a spouse, son or daughter, or other loved ones find that rather than carrying the burden of being the caregiver, they can now return to be that special loved one such as a wife, husband, son, or daughter.

How do you know if out-of-home care is necessary? Here are some issues to consider:

- Is the medical team indicating in-home hospice is indicated? If so, does the loved one want to be at home to the very end?
- Is twenty-four-hour caregiving support necessary? Are there family members available for this?
- Are family caregivers able to turn, lift, and move the ill person?
- Can family caregivers also manage other family or work responsibilities?

- Can the home accommodate things such as a hospital bed, wheelchairs, or oxygen?
- Is the bathroom accessible? If not, is remodeling possible?
- Sometimes the caregiver is elderly or otherwise not strong enough to provide care.
- Is good pain and symptom management possible at home?

Pain management

The goal of pain management is to improve quality of life. A common fear and point of anxiety is the thought that you or your loved one may die with uncontrolled pain, but a good medication plan removes this as a concern. Many individuals have said they are no longer afraid of death but fear uncontrolled pain. There is a big difference between end-of-life uses of opioids and addiction. Opioid use at the end of life is simply a controlled plan of care. Any dependence can be managed easily. Addiction is the abuse of opioids in an uncontrolled manner and not at the end of life.

Your loved one may show signs of needing pain medication without necessarily asking for it. These signs include:

- Restlessness
- Irritability
- Difficulty sleeping
- Loss of appetite
- Inability to concentrate
- Wincing or grimacing especially when being moved
- Limited activity and socialization

Depending on the underlying illness, the type of pain and how it feels physically can vary. Some pain originates from the center of the body where the stomach, colon, liver, and kidneys reside. This visceral pain is sometimes described as cramping, deep pressure, or gnawing.

Some pain may start in the bones or musculoskeletal area and feel like a deep pressure, pounding, or aching pain. There also is the pain that originates where nerves are impacted. This can be the peripheral or central nervous system. Pain is described as sharp, electric, burning, throbbing, and never relenting. Opioids are used for all types of pain and can be effective. However, the origin or type of pain may also benefit by a secondary medication that specifically targets that area.

Pain management—principals and benefits:

- The use of pain medication should not be avoided if prescribed by the doctor.
- Pain relief makes activities easier.
- Improves sleep.
- Reduces stress, which has health benefits.
- Allows the mind to focus on other things in life.
- Building a tolerance to the medication is normal.
- Physical tolerance is not addiction.
- Physical need for pain relief is different than a psychological need.

Pain is described as "what the person says it is." Each person has his or her own pain tolerance levels as well as expressions of pain. When assessing pain, have the person tell you the level of their pain on a scale of 1-10. Pain that is not controlled can lead to muscle tension to protect the area that is hurting.

Give medication on a regular schedule to maintain a consistent level of pain relief. Other medications can be used for "break-through" pain. Most pain can be controlled with oral medications, but other options are available. The health-care provider or hospice staff should monitor the medication plan.

Physical side effects of pain medication may include:

- Physical tolerance
- Sleepiness
- Nausea and vomiting
- Constipation
- Lower respiratory rate

Nonmedical techniques can greatly assist in managing pain. They provide ways family members can help. These include:

- Maintain a calm environment.
- Play soothing music; the type of music of personal choice.
- Suggest distracting activities such as TV, movies, visitors.
- Schedule activities during the optimal pain control.
- Gentle massage of head, hands, and feet can be relaxing. This can lower pain levels.
- Guided imagery.
- Heat or cold packs.

Donny was a sixteen-year-old foster child at a hospital one hundred miles from home. His cancer was widespread, and he was in severe pain. His anxiety level was high. He was scared. He had been at the hospital many times over the past years, so he was well known by the doctors and nurses and well loved. There was great frustration in attempting to manage his complex pain. One staff member who was Christian knew that Donny did not know Jesus. With a policy forbidding evangelizing, she was anxious for him to know the comfort of Christ but unable to speak to him about it. However, God had another plan for Donny. One afternoon a teenage girl who knew of Donny went to visit him. She shared the story of God's plan of salvation and the infinite grace and love He had for Donny. Donny accepted the invitation to bring Christ into his life. He was filled with joy and relief. The staff was amazed at his peaceful countenance. Within the next twenty-four hours they watched his need for pain medication dramatically drop. When asked by the doctors and staff what changed, Donny responded, "I now have Jesus in my life." Donny died comfortably and in peace.

The right to die from a Christian perspective

Because making the decision to end life-support is so consequential and irreversible, it deserves an in-depth look, not only into the decision to stop life-support at the very end of life, but also into physician-assisted suicide, and what we might call "compassionate" euthanasia.

To understand this better, it will be helpful to learn a little bit about medical ethics. Dr. Thomas Beauchamp and Dr. James Childress developed a set of bioethical guidelines that are considered the gold standard by many. They divided the ethical treatment by doctors of their patients into four categories they refer to as "pillars."

- Autonomy: Respecting the decision-making capacities of autonomous persons; enabling individuals to make reasoned informed choices.
- Beneficence: This considers the balancing of benefits of treatment against the risks and costs; the health-care professional should act in a way that benefits the patient.
- Nonmaleficence: Avoiding the causation of harm; the healthcare professional should not harm the patient. All treatment involves some harm, even if minimal, but the harm should not be disproportionate to the benefits of treatment.

- Justice: Distributing benefits, risks, and costs fairly; the notion that patients in similar positions should be treated in a similar manner.[7]

Applying biblical principles to Beauchamp and Childress's ethical pillars:

- Autonomy: God gives us free will; therefore, we should respect the choices your loved ones make if they are capable of making decisions. For the family, this can be a great relief. "Now choose life, so that you and your children may live and that you may love the Lord your God, listen to his voice, and hold fast to him" (Deuteronomy 30:19b–20a NIV). This passage implies we also have the freedom to choose life or death.

- Beneficence: Take actions that will benefit your loved one considering all the information you have available. "The greatest among you must be a servant"(Matthew 23:11 NLT) As servants, we must always strive to benefit those we serve.

- Nonmaleficence: Do no harm. Even though medical treatments may cause pain in the short term, the goal is to make life better. "For the commandments say, 'You must not commit adultery. You must not murder. You must not steal. You must not covet.' These—and other such commandments— are summed up in this one commandment: 'Love your neighbor as yourself. Love does no wrong to others, so love fulfills the requirements of God's law'" (Romans 13:9–10 NLT). True love does not do harm.

- Justice: Fairness to all regardless of their race, gender, or social status. To this we might apply the concept of futility. We are not in violation of biblical principles if we do not continue treatments that will do absolutely nothing to benefit the ill

---

[7] Tom L. Beauchamp, and James F. Childress, *Principles of biomedical ethics* (New York: Oxford University Press, 2003).

person especially when a shortage of these treatments will cause harm to someone whose prognosis is more hopeful. This is not as clear in the United States as it is in some countries where medical supplies and treatments must be rationed. "Do what is right whenever possible. Learn to do good. Seek justice. Help the oppressed. Defend the cause of orphans. Fight for the rights of widows" (Isaiah 1:17 NLT). In all cases, do what is right.

Applying ethics to real-life scenarios can be complicated by:

- Wishes of different family members
- The mental status of the ill person
- Cultural beliefs
- Religious beliefs
- Past experiences

Physician assisted suicide and compassionate euthanasia

Several US states currently allow for physician-assisted suicide (PAS.) PAS has several names given by its supporters, such as "Death with Dignity," "Aid in Dying," and "Assisted Death." Compassionate euthanasia is a decision made for someone who cannot speak for himself or herself, to be withdrawn from life-sustaining support, such as feeding tubes and oxygen, when the ill person is not facing imminent death but may never recover to what might be referred to as a good quality of life. This differs from the withdrawal of life support at the end of life.

The primary reason people choose PAS is fear they will lose control over their lives. They don't want to become dependent on others, which they see as a loss of dignity, especially if they should need help with feeding and toileting. They fear what they expect to be a painful experience as a pointless waste.

Dr. Ira Byock is a well-known palliative-care physician and medical ethicist. He is the author of several books on palliative care and end-of-life decisions. He says that a rush to end life support or the use of physician-assisted suicide is a failure of the medical system to provide the proper care to the ill person and the family. Their needs were not met. They did not feel the support of the medical system, nor, perhaps, their friends and family. They did not have trust. Dr. Byock challenges the pro-PAS argument that PAS is death with dignity. "When people are coming to the end of life, dignity is held by the family and community. Dignity resides in the relationship. When we become unable to care for ourselves, dignity is maintained by the loving family who cares for us."[8]

How to decide when to end life support: There may come a time when nothing can be done to comfort the ill person or support his or her life. Ask yourself and the doctor these questions:

- Is there a zero percent chance that the life support measures can save the person?
- Could life support help through a temporary medical crisis?
- Is the condition expected as part of the end of a terminal illness?
- Will more treatment make the person more comfortable?

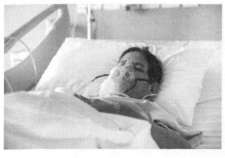

Death may be imminent as a result of the illness. Heroic measures may be useless, or worse, harmful at this time. You and your medical team may feel this is the time to let your loved one go. Pray for peace and guidance. This is usually a good time to reach out to family.

---

[8] Ira Byock, MD http://www.cbsnews.com/news/ending-life-barbara-mancini-end-of-life-debate/October 19, 2014 Correspondent Anderson Cooper.

Biblical guiding principles to help with the decision to end life-support:

- God knows our hearts.
- Our motivations are important.
- Our bodies are gifts from God, and we must be good stewards of them.
- God is the giver of life. It is not ours to take.
- The Bible does not give poor quality of life as a reason to purposefully end life.
- We do not have to do what is futile.

Dying is not a walk in the park. There is physical and emotional pain for sure. Finding value in throwing up or waiting to be attended to in a nursing home cannot be transformed into good times. It is understandable that someone may choose to die before the Lou Gehrig's disease gets worse, or the family savings are spent on expenses not covered by insurance. If only we could look at the experience from outside ourselves. If only we could see from God's eyes, we would find hope.

The end of life holds great value for God. God can and does use that time for good. Our greatest hope is in God's promise for eternal life. This is *the* promise through Christ.

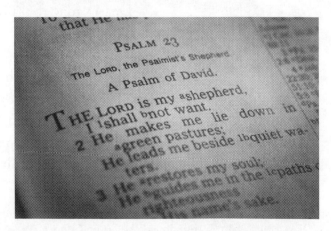

12

A FAMILY EXPERIENCE—
SANDY'S STORY

My name is Sandy, and I'd like to tell you my story about my dad and his passing several years ago in 2007. I come from a large family of six kids—a mom and dad, you know, a large Catholic family. Mom and dad were married for sixty-four years—a long time. We were a fairly close-knit family of the 1960s—at least what was considered close-knit for that time.

I can't really say my Dad and I were close while I grew up and in my early adult years. He worked for more than fifty years for the Union Pacific. And throughout my childhood, my mom was both a stay-at-home mom and one who also worked outside the home.

When my dad came home from work, he usually sat down to have one beer while he watched the news, and my mom saw to it that we were to be quiet during this time so he could de-stress from work. This is how it worked, and it worked well.

After I grew up, I reflected about my childhood and saw that my dad wasn't there for me emotionally a lot of the time. Of course, there were highlights and times especially created for making memories, and most of that was good. He wasn't there because he traveled a lot in his job. And I was angry with my dad for a long time, a subtle smoldering anger that I couldn't put my finger on. My dad knew at some level that I was angry with him but didn't know what to make of it or how to end it or what to say.

During my teen and early adult years, I will have to say my dad and I were pretty distant. We were equally stubborn, distant, and just didn't know what to say to each other. Once I moved out of the house, and I was on my own, it went on this way for five to ten years or so. At some point, my feelings started to soften toward my dad because when I would go home, he was glad to see me. You know how that is? Distance makes the heart grow fonder type of thing. It's also called maturing and growing up.

In 1997, I decided I wanted a relationship with Jesus Christ. It was both a difficult and beautiful time in my life. As I became closer to God, both my mom and dad struggled with my decision. They initially felt betrayed because I didn't choose Catholicism. They felt that I let them down, and I felt like they had let me down because no one had shown me how to have a personal relationship with God. As my parents and I navigated these spiritual waters, it was slow going with the three of us. I vowed to keep an open heart about their feelings and questions, and they did the same. They tried hard not to judge me, asked questions, and they agreed to visit my church with me to see what it was all about.

We talked about the similarities in our faith and decided that this was what God wanted us to concentrate on. They both enjoyed hearing my pastor very much. I love that they were willing to do that; it took courage, love, and openness about Christianity outside of Catholicism. I also increased the time I spent with them going to Mass to celebrate their faith. In the end, God provided a peace among us three that no one could understand. God was faithful to give us peace, understanding, and a willingness to share our faith with each other. As this increased, our friendship went off the chart! This is something I cherish in my memories of them. None of their other children have these memories and because of that, I get melancholy when I think about it. My parents saw that, at last, I wanted to know who they were as people, not just Mom and Dad. Going to celebrate Mass was the one thing they wanted from their children—it was so easy for me to give them this small thing for everything they had given me.

My dad was a stoic but quiet man. He always kept his word, always tried to be honorable, and, in my memories, never lied to his wife or children. As I grew in my relationship with God, I would ask, "God, what do you see in my dad?" I would see pictures of him being courageous, quietly, without any fanfare, and not asking for attention. And when I saw that I said, 'God, what else don't I see in my dad?' Bits and pieces would come to my mind. At times Dad would be funny when he would try to make us laugh, or when he wanted to say something, but he was hesitant because he didn't know what kind of reaction I would give him.

I wrote a tribute to each one of my parents. It took me six months to do it because every time I sat down to write something, something negative would get into the mix. I said to myself, *It's not going to have one negative word in it.* So, by the time Christmas came, I handed a four-page tribute to each one of my parents. In it I tried to validate them by recognizing them as people; some of their dreams didn't happen—dreams they had to change because of the children coming along, lack of money, or maybe where God had put them. But I wanted to acknowledge that some of their dreams did not come true, and I was sorry for that. The same thing for my mom but in a different way and a different tribute. They were both crying when they read it. My dad told me many months later, "I still look at it when I need to lighten up."

During and after 2004, the health of both my parents deteriorated. Mom was beginning to seriously decline into dementia, and Dad ended up with cancer. He had benign melanoma for more than twenty years and periodically had lesions removed by laser. However, this tumor was golf ball-sized and was malignant. After eight weeks of radiation and a new cocktail of pills every day, he was showing great fatigue from the experience. Of course, he wasn't prepared emotionally for the ordeal with cancer treatment—no one is. This type of radiation had his head mask bolted to a table during the procedure. If he had a breathing problem or nausea, he could have choked. Slowly his appetite went away, then his sense of smell. He lost his hair. This was the same time that my mother's dementia started her decline. And so, my dad was dealing with both things at the same time. He never really complained, whined, or greatly expressed aloud what he was feeling. This was his way of being a man and fighting the good fight. (When he finished radiation, he wanted to keep the mask as a memento. My mother said no!) What he was going through and what he was doing made him a hero in my eyes. That was the first time I'd ever seen that in him, and I told him that.

After the radiation, he had about three years before they found cancer again in his stomach and some of his other of organs. He said to me, "I'm eighty-four; your mom's taken care of. I know all of you will take care of her." He was hanging on so much for her. I began to see how much my dad loved my mom. Kids don't often get to see how much their parents love each other. At least not with that generation.

In 2006, we had gotten my mom and dad moved out of their house into assisted living. It was hard because my mom's Alzheimer's was advancing quickly, and it was traumatizing for her to leave her place of safety. By the time we got them moved, he knew. He wrote me a card and said, "You know, I've lost her. Take care of her; it's time to go home." This was so hard on him—losing her as his wife at the same time he was having terminal cancer. He said, "God, I'm ready, I'm so ready. I wanted to be here to take care of her, but she's not here."

I began to see how brave he really was, and I realized my dad has a strong faith in God. I just hadn't been able to see it. I really hadn't been able to see it. And it was because of my own critical spirit. It is something that I am still healing from, and it plagues my family and many others. No one is truly immune. But we can be healed from it. That's why God says He will take me from Glory to Glory. I think that's about growing up in God. He just keeps taking you from one season, and you grow some; then you go on to the next hurdle, and you grow some, and on and on.

In one of our bedside conversations, I said, "I wish I could have a do-over with you, Dad," through my tears. He just said with a smile, "Don't we all!" We would have such a different relationship. Then he looked at me and said, "Don't worry. We will." And I knew what he meant. I realized that this time with him brought him joy, and if I had never decided to let Jesus into my life, we wouldn't have spent that time in the way we did—with honesty, love, grief, sorrow, and sometimes joy and laughter.

One of the things Dad said to me while he was dying, and in a letter to me, was that my new relationship with God was one of the highlights of his life and that he had thanked God over and over that I had come home. He said he would pray for his other children to do the same after he was gone because he knew that not all would make it to Heaven. When you're heading toward death, and you get to a state of vulnerability, it's precious. When I read the Twenty-Third Psalm to him and we prayed out of the Bible, he would just get weepy. It's like, "God I need you so much; please be here with me."

Christmas 2006 was one that felt horrific. He was weak, emaciated, and at that point near death.

He was on various medicines and, at some point, had been given a bit too much. During that Christmas Day he became unusually awake and yet was not mentally or emotionally present. He kept trying to get out of bed to go somewhere, and we knew he couldn't be left alone. So, during that Christmas day, we took turns sitting by his bedside. This turned out to be for nearly thirty hours. He would talk about this task or he needed to go to that place. He didn't really know who we were or sometimes whether anyone was there at the bedside or not. There is some mild disagreement among us siblings about what was going on. He received a larger than normal dose of one of his medicines. But there was nothing that would cause hallucinations.

There is a phenomenon that hospice workers call processing life. People about to die often have a life review. They consider it a part of taking care of the business of wrapping up a life. Not everyone goes through this. It is something they consider spiritual or a deep part of the soul getting ready to leave.

I ask you, who wouldn't do this if he or she has time to do so? My dad was a guy all about taking care of business. He spent his work life as an auditor! He and my mom even planned out, on paper, every summer trip we went on while growing up. He was so organized that he made it extraordinarily easy to deal with funeral arrangements because he had them paid for a decade before along with a living trust! My dad knew how (and it was part of his DNA) to take care of business and conclude it. He wouldn't leave anything undone that he was responsible for, if it was within his power.

So, this is what I believe: during these thirty-some odd hours that he stayed awake, he went through his entire life. He lived a lot of things over again. Going to the bank. Watering his tomatoes. Going on a trip. Talking about money matters. Talking to that person up there in the corner near the ceiling as if the person was his friend. He was engaged, talking to people, doing business, walking around (in his mind) doing stuff, and on and on. I think the medication freed up whatever inhibitions he might have had at that time and let him relax enough to deal with what he needed to do. But he wasn't hallucinating. I've seen people hallucinate, and that wasn't it. It was an enigma that isn't explainable to the intellect. Those who won't open their heart to God's spirituality don't understand that God loves to interact with us in supernatural ways—the only way that kind of person can explain it is with the intellect.

All of us got to sit with him. My sister and I went up for our three hours and were sitting by the bed, He just looked at me, then turned his head to my sister and said, (without his dentures in) "You know life, it's just like a bowl full of cherries." The tears were streaming down our eyes when we said, "You know, Dad, you're right. Life *is* just like a bowl full of cherries." In his weakness and emotional state, he was open like a child. It was beautiful to me. In his weakness he said things that he would never say otherwise in his normal state. He was gentle and vulnerable.

He passed in January. I got the call from my sister, who asked if I could go to him. She was broken and unable to go. When I got to the foster home, he couldn't talk or move, but I laid my hand on his forehead and anointed him. I sang him a worship song, which I had never done before. I felt that all I needed to do at that point was to tell him to go. He was staring at me very intently as if he knew he had to listen to what I said. "It's time to go home to be with Jesus tonight now, Dad. It's okay. We all love you, and you will be in our hearts forever. But we want you to go now. It will just be a blink of your eye before Mom follows you. You need to be looking for her as soon as you get there. That's your job now. Keep on the lookout for her when you get home because you know how sometimes she gets lost. I'm going to go now, because it's time for you to leave." Then I left him as if I would see him the following week. My heart was literally breaking in a million pieces. I couldn't breathe when I got to my car. It was finally sinking in. But I wouldn't trade those moments for anything. Some might say, "What does all that get you? Why put yourself through misery?" I think those who don't say goodbye or I love you or thank you for being this person in my life, all miss out on the most important point of life: To know that you are loved.

The morning he died the gal running the foster home called and said, "Your dad just passed." I thanked her for all she had done for him in the last few weeks of his life. She was a very special person— an angel, really, with skin on. When I hung up, I just said, "Thank you, Jesus." It was a bright, sunny, beautiful Sunday January morning. And I said, "You are walking into the gates of Heaven right now, and you're leaving that old body behind. You never have to have it again. I'm so happy for you, Dad." Before the avalanche of sorrow hit—just before that—I was very happy for him. I knew he was free.

At his funeral, we all were pretty good until the end. Then, of course, some of us were emotional and some held it in till they were in private. I read my tribute to my dad at the funeral because it was something I wanted people to know about my dad. He deserved it.

My mom's story? It was much more difficult to live through. I know they are both free of their diseased, hurting, and sick bodies. I see them as young and laughing again. Dancing the Jitterbug. Full of dreams again. And I know this time, unlike our life here on earth, all their dreams will come true.

13

LATER STAGES

O Lord, you have examined my heart
and know everything about me.
You know when I sit down or stand up.
You know my every thought when far away.
You chart the path ahead of me
and tell me where to stop and rest.
Every moment you know where I am.
(Psalm 139:1–3 NLT)

As the end looks like it is getting closer, reality is beginning to set in. You may have had a long journey with your loved ones, praying for a healing until now. Feelings of grief and fear may hit you hard as you begin to anticipate your loss. You may ask why again. Why has the journey been so difficult?

People react differently to the final days. Sometimes there is denial even though there are many outward signs that death is imminent. If the later stage has been long or painful, family members may secretly hope death will come soon so that their loved one doesn't have to suffer anymore. You may still be waiting for the person to get better. It is okay to pray for healing because God wants to answer this kind of prayer. If we look for His miracles, we will find them, but they may be different from what we first expect. Some people do recover to the great amazement of their doctors, or, more commonly, they outlive their predicted time. There are other types of healing, such as emotional healing, relational healing, and spiritual healing.

Many people feel worthless when their illness progresses to the point where they are dependent on others for their everyday care. This is the part we fear the most. Jesus sees you as a whole person. You never become worthless to Him. No matter what happens in the last stages of life, God still loves you, and he loves your loved ones! He sees through all sicknesses, disabilities, and conditions to see your heart and soul that He created. He loves you through all stages of living and dying.

What happens when someone dies? No one journey is exactly the same as another. Many people stay physically active to within weeks or days of their death. Some are still walking hours before the end. It can be gradual over months or an almost daily decline. Sometimes the disease seems to hit several crisis times followed by relatively quiet periods. Usually, there is a gradual state of debility over a period of days. At the very end, the ill person may sleep a lot or go into a coma. Breathing may become erratic.

Your loved one may experience a loss of appetite and thirst leading to refusing to eat anything as the intestines cease to function. This is a sign that the body is shutting down. Family members can feel desperate for the ill person to eat, fearing that death will come from starvation. Trying to force eating may cause discomfort. The main cause of death is vital organ failure of the heart, brain, kidneys, lungs, or liver. For some illnesses, bleeding and/or infections can be complications leading to death.

Symptoms are often related to the specific illness. Those with neuromuscular diseases may experience a progression of symptoms related to swallowing, speech, mobility, and elimination. Those with heart failure may experience shortness of breath, wheezing, swelling, and increased heart rate. People with dementia, such as Alzheimer's disease, may exhibit difficulty swallowing, stop speaking or speak with few words, and have incontinence.

Pain is the symptom many fear. However, not everyone has a painful death. Once again, it depends on the condition and the individual's tolerance level. The use of strong pain medications at the end of life is not unusual. They greatly reduce the suffering in the last minutes and hours. Some medications induce a deep sedation to avoid excruciating pain. Sometimes they are increased when the decision is made to remove life-support because this may be uncomfortable to the ill person. Medications such as morphine reduce symptoms of air hunger for those with respiratory conditions. Does morphine hasten death? This is a common question; however, studies show that properly used morphine does not hasten death. It can help relieve pulmonary edema, which is common at the end of life.

In the last hours, the ill person may develop a rattling sound when breathing. This is called Cheyne-stoking and is caused by secretions in the back of the throat that the ill person is unable to clear. Sometimes suctioning and/or medications help, but this is more for the benefit of the family. In the last hours, breathing becomes irregular with deep breathes followed by moments of no breath. The ill person is probably not aware of this. The face may look gaunt as the muscles completely relax. The hands and feet may appear blotchy and mottled and be cool to the touch. Breathing gradually slows and then stops. Death may occur with eyes open or closed. The face may appear pale soon after death. With today's more advanced symptom management, death is usually peaceful.

Keeping the vigil is defined as one or more persons staying with the ill person until the end of life comes. This is a time for friends and family to come and say goodbye. It can also be a time of reunion and reconciliation among families. Family members may take turns sitting with the ill person, allowing the others to eat or rest. This can bring the family together especially if end-of-life decisions have already been made and communicated. Family members can comfort each other. Participating in the care, by putting a cool cloth on the forehead or rubbing the hands and feet, helps the family feel they can assist in some way. This is an intimate time that family and friends will not forget.

Sometimes the ill person dies suddenly just when everyone has left the room. Try not to let this haunt you. Consider the possibility that they may have given up purposefully perhaps to protect loved ones from what they perceive as a devastating experience.

What does it mean to have a good death? Some ideas are:

- Being free of pain and fear.
- Having family gathered around the dying person singing, praying, or saying farewell.
- Have only a few people present.
- Some might want those who are there to eat popcorn or have toast with something to drink, as one person shared with us.
- Some want to die at home while others prefer to be elsewhere.

Those who can share the last moments with their loved one report that it was a profound experience and that they were glad they could "see them off." As sad, frightening, and stressful as the

end of life can be, it can also be beautiful. The Lord is with the dying person, and many people can feel this. It brings friends and family together with the goal of giving loving comfort to the ill person and their loved ones. Prayer is often accepted even by non-Christian family and friends. This experience can bring us closer to God. It brings out the best in us. The service you do out of love for each other is never in vain. Who knows, it may have eternal significance!

Where do we go when we die? Seven out of ten Americans believe we go to Heaven.[9] It is comforting to think our loved one's suffering is over, that he or she is in a perfect place with all the loved ones who went on before. If you are a Christian, you may be worried about your loved one's faith. You may not be convinced your loved one will go to Heaven if you doubt that he or she accepted Christ.

What a blessing: from Sue's memoirs. Phil was actively dying. His wife, Margaret, had recently shared with me her concern about Phil's faith. Was he really a believer? Did he know Jesus? Or was he simply accompanying her to church? She couldn't imagine sharing eternity without him. A couple of days later, as his wife sat at his side, I visited them. The nurses described him as highly anxious. As I sat on his bed he dramatically reached up with both arms. He said he saw Jesus. As if alone, he sought His grace and declared his love of Christ. He thanked Him for his wife. What more could his wife want! She now was ready to let him go. He died a few hours later.

---

[9] Caryle Murphy, "Most Americans believe in Heaven … and Hell," http://pewrsr.ch/1O1cYWD, May 30, 2019.

A biblical look at Heaven and other things

Is Heaven an actual place? Yes, the Bible tells us it is a real place and has numerous passages talking about it.

There is more than enough room in my Father's home. (John 14:2 NLT)

Heaven is something to look forward to. We will have new bodies. There will be no more sin, no more sickness, and no more tears. And there will be no more suffering!

He will take these weak mortal bodies of ours and change them into glorious bodies like his own. (Philippians 3:21 NLT)

He will remove all of their sorrows, and there will be no more death or sorrow or crying or pain. (Revelation 21:4a NLT)

It is not the end but the beginning of everlasting life. Heaven is immensely beautiful. It is our true home.

It shone with the glory of God and sparkled like a precious stone—like jasper as clear as crystal. (Revelation 21:11. NLT)

We will be with Christ.

> For he raised us from the dead along with Christ and
> seated us with him in the heavenly realms because we
> are united with Christ Jesus. (Ephesians 2:6 NLT)

This is the Good News! God promises that if we accept Jesus as our Savior, we will live with Him in Paradise forever.

What about Hell?

Unfortunately, it is a real place too. How can we understand Hell in light of a loving God? God wants no one to be lost. Heaven is where God is. Hell is where He is not. C. S. Lewis said, "I willingly believe that the damned are, in one sense, successful, rebels to the end; that the doors of Hell are locked on the inside."[10]

> It is by God's Grace that we are saved. For if you
> confess with your mouth that Jesus is Lord and
> believe in your heart that God raised him from the
> dead, you will be saved. (Romans 10:9 NLT)

God works up to the point of death to bring us to Christ. God is merciful and never sends an innocent person to Hell. Many theologians believe that children and mentally challenged adults, for example, go straight to Heaven. Remember that God is good and more loving than we can imagine! Your faithful prayers may have saved your loved one!

Story of a 104-year-old hospice patient. Family members of Evelyn just could not figure out why she seemed to hang on to life for such a long time even though she was languishing in a bed, unable to care for herself. She confided to a hospice volunteer she was afraid to die. "God will be angry with me and might even send me to Hell,"

---

[10] C. S. Lewis, *The Problem of Pain* (New York: Macmillan, 1962).

she said. Gradually Evelyn revealed a secret she had carried all her life. When she was a teenager, she had done "something" with a boy. The hospice volunteer comforted her by saying, "Sweetie, if God keeps you from Heaven over that, none of us will get there either." She died a few days later in peace.

> Your unfailing love, Oh LORD, is as vast as the heavens; your faithfulness reaches beyond the clouds. (Psalm 36:5 NLT)

Each person has been given a soul.

> For then the dust will return to the earth, and the spirit will return to God who gave it. (Ecclesiastes 12:7 NLT)

When a loved one slips into a coma or when dementia has progressed to the phase when they seem like vegetables, they are not dead or gone yet! At the very least their soul is still alive as Jesus implies: "Don't be afraid of those who want to kill your body; they cannot touch your soul" (Matthew 10:28a NLT). Talk to the ill person just as you would if he or she was coherent. People who recover from comas often report they could hear words spoken to them.

God did not want physical death for us originally, but humans brought it upon themselves through Adam and Eve. God will use the dying process for *glorious* things. Your faith and courage through your dying process will have a huge impact on others! God can and does use people *even* when they are in a coma, have lost their ability to speak, or have lost touch with reality.

> How we thank God, who gives us victory over sin and death through Jesus Christ our Lord! So, my

dear brothers and sisters, be strong and steady, always enthusiastic about the Lord's work, for you know that nothing you do for the Lord is ever useless. (1 Corinthians 15:57–58 NLT)

Grief may come and go, but when the end comes the grief will become extremely intense. This is the time for surrender. This is the time to admit you are not in control. Let your heavenly Father comfort you. Talk to Him and turn to scripture. Let Him be in control. You can trust Him. He won't let you down.

Jesus will *never* leave you or forsake you. We have the wonderful promise of Heaven after we die. After the suffering will come Paradise. Our lives are so short compared to eternity. Make the most of every minute of life here on earth to be a shining light for Him. You will be richly blessed.

14

ETERNAL PURPOSES

When this happens—when our perishable earthly bodies have been transformed into heavenly bodies that will never die—then at last the Scriptures will come true: Death is swallowed up in victory. O death, where is your victory? O death, where is your sting? For sin is the sting that results in death, and the law gives sin its power. How we thank God, who gives us victory over sin and death through Jesus Christ our Lord! (1 Corinthians 15:54–57 NLT)

Original sin brought death, but Jesus conquered sin and death on the cross! Death is swallowed up in victory and the scriptures will come true! Does this apply to us today? We are still suffering and dying, so how can this be a victory now? What does victory look like?

Death is both a bad nightmare and a magnificent healing. It is the ultimate healing that lasts for eternity. The experience of walking a loved one through a terminal illness changes us. Something at the soul level makes us more connected to others.

God uses the end of life to heal and grow those who loved and cared for the ill person. Suddenly, many of life's difficulties seem small in comparison. He uses it to influence future generations. He can use it to make us better people than we were before. We can become more compassionate, giving, and less fearful of the future. Families come closer together.

> **Leon's story.** Leon was a scientist, well-educated, and successful. He was quiet about religion but gave the impression he didn't have a faith. His wife and several of his children were Christians. On the day he died, his children, grandchildren, and his wife gathered around him. After several hours of keeping the vigil, his granddaughter and her husband, Tom, left to take their baby home. But on the way, Tom had an overwhelming urge to go back to the hospital. And so, they returned. Tom asked if he could pray for Leon. He held his hand and offered a simple invitation for him to accept Christ as his Savior. Leon squeezed his hand to say yes! Thirty minutes later, he died. Leon lived a good life helping others. He left the world a better place than when he found it. And best of all, he was saved!

The Lord wants no one to be lost. Salvation is available to anyone. God is a gentleman and will not force himself on you. Jesus already paid the price for you. If you have never accepted Christ as your Savior, you can do that now.

> For God so loved the world that he gave his one and only Son, that whoever believes in him shall not perish but have eternal life. (John 3:16 NIV)

God made this easy. All you must do is open your heart. He will do the rest. Proclaim that He is Lord, and you will be saved. If you can't speak, like Leon, don't worry, He knows your heart.

> If you confess with your mouth that Jesus is Lord and believe in your heart that God raised him from the dead, you will be saved. (Romans 10:9 NLT)

God wants us to trust Him that He will use our lives for His good purposes. We cannot see the cosmic impact our lives have on the world, but we must believe that there is one. Our suffering is not just about us, nor is it just a waste. God has called you for just such a time as this. He equips you to feel and respond with more understanding than ever before. Sharing in someone's end-of-life experience can be one of the most intimate, most loving, and most profound experiences of all.

God values us during all phases of our lives. Many will not be aware of the work God is doing, in part because the experience is so stressful. But He is working! Some even find salvation. Have you ever noticed how a dying person seems to become more and more gentle, humble, and loving? This is no accident. Many people are affected by the illness and death of one person. That is why we call it "God's symphony orchestra." God weaves emotions and events beautifully and powerfully like music from an orchestra with the ill person as the center note.

"The message is that love begets love and fear begets fear. To this we see that our part of helping our loved ones through their time of fear is by giving them the greatest dose of love in word and deed that we can muster." (Paraphrased)[11]

---

[11] William H. Ammon, *Walking Our Loved One Home: Love Never Fails* (Morris Pub., 1995).

Could our faith, which often seems to grow more intense as death gets more imminent, be part of God's plan to refine us like gold? We are never perfect on this earth, but these last hours may bring us the closest to being perfect that we will know until we go to our real home. Could living with a life-threatening illness and then dying with faith in Him be our ultimate victory in life?

Could this process of healing, reconciliation, intense love, and the salvation of many, be a reason why there is suffering in the world? Just like Job, who chose God despite his terrible suffering, we can draw closer and closer to Christ despite this otherwise terrible experience. Could this be God's ultimate victory for humankind?

There is no beauty in death. It is the love of God that is beautiful. There is no victory in suffering. It is the movement of God and the faithfulness of His followers even under the burden of great suffering that is victorious.

Every day is known to God. God has a purpose and a plan for our lives. This does not change just because an illness changes our view of things.

God has a master plan that includes us but is much bigger than we are.

Trusting Him is our only pathway to a full and dignified death.

God values us during all phases of our lives.

People do not lose their worth when they

become sick or incapacitated.

Three things will last forever—faith, hope, and love—and the greatest of these is love. (1 Corinthians 13:13 NLT)

EPILOGUE
The Role of the Faith Community

Where better than in the church should we be able to talk about facing the possibility of the end of life? As Christians, it is a transition to our real life in eternity to be with our heavenly Father, the believers who have gone before us, and the angelic heavenly host. And yet the thought of leaving loved ones behind, even if temporarily, brings on great sadness. The fear that it will be a painful death is overwhelming. The fear that we will be alone or dependent on others only adds to the anxiety. This is true for everyone; however, as Christians, we have been given the gifts of grace, prayer, peace, and the presence of Christ to comfort us. Christ uses His faithful community to serve those facing these challenging times, and that includes the family. Some churches offer Stephen Ministry, homebound ministries,

prayer groups, prayer shawls, and comfort quilts. One parish closes its Mass with the pastor inviting everyone taking communion to the sick and homebound to come forward to be blessed. He reminds them that they are bringing prayers that are from the whole parish along with the communion.

One way a congregation can begin the conversation among its members is to have speakers or workshops on end-of-life planning, which everyone should do earlier in life. Many pastors ask members to complete a form on funeral plans, which is then kept in the church office. Parish nurses often invite in speakers on a variety of topics such as "Tips on Visiting Shut-ins," "What is Hospice Care," and "Estate Planning."

For those seeking an educational support format, the Wilderness Journey Ministries' nine-week series is available. It comes divided into three three-week series called journeys. (See appendix 1) These can be used as outreach programs to the community.

The faith community can also play an important role in helping with practical needs such as bringing meals, shopping, running errands, and providing respite care for caregivers. Several website tools are used by families and/or congregations in organizing such care. Once it is set up online, a list of needs with possible dates can be created. Church members can go online and sign up with tasks they would help with. These programs reduce a lot of phone calling to family members. Two popular sites are www.carecalendar.org and www.caringbridge.org. Families become informed of medical changes, challenges, and/or crises.

These can be times of spiritual questions as families try to cope with changes. Spiritual care counselors (chaplains) are there to listen, ask questions, and when possible, help when these issues or questions arise. The individual's own church pastor certainly has a place and may know the family well already. Bringing of the Lord's Supper or communion to the bedside for the individual and family to partake can be an intimate and memorable time. The end of life is a spiritual time, and many families surround their loved one and lift him or her up in prayer. Some families will take turns reading the scriptures and singing to their loved ones. It is a powerful time. It is God's time.

Despite all these offerings, many are uncomfortable talking about their fears and concerns about end of life. Visitors do not know what to say or fear it will be too emotional. As Christians, we can get over this barrier through prayer and the help of Jesus Christ.

The key is not worrying about what to say but rather to simply listen. Let them decide what the conversation will focus on during the time together. Ask them to share something about their lives such as where they grow up or what good memories they cherish. You can also ask them what their greatest concern is, which will tell you what is important to them. Many who are ill find themselves doing some "life review," which can be healing. This can be a powerful and satisfying experience for you. Each time you realize the Lord is in charge, you can relax and be "present." Each time we serve the Lord, we begin with our relationship with Christ. As we serve, we begin to realize we are getting closer and closer to Him.

Spiritual care is more than religious practices and traditions. It is the Holy Spirit at work in us and through us. It is those times when individuals feel connected to us. This comes when fellow Christians express their concern and empathy for those facing a life-threatening illness. One may feel anxious on the first visit, but remember Psalm 46:10: "Be still and know that I am God." Lift your anxieties to God in prayer before you go on your visit. Initially, it involves more listening than anything else. Let the individual or family set the tone of the visit. Those who seem to have a need to share tend to want to tell their story about how they got to this point, initial symptoms, tests, and doctors, etc. It is as if they are trying to make sense of the situation. It is their attempt to understand "why." One needs to simply listen, maybe asking questions to clarify the information. However, many illnesses are complex, which makes understanding difficult. As you become more comfortable, you bring a "comforting presence," and words are not always necessary. It has been said, "If you do not understand my silence, you do not understand my words" (author, Elbert Hubbard). A parish nurse wrote, "To realize God's presence, one needs to practice quietness. It enables us to hear the voice of God in one another, to see the face of God in another, to be in touch with the pain or confusion that is their life. God's presence is made known through us, His people."[12] Not every visit needs to include a deep discussion. Even a social visit reduces the sense of loneliness. A quiet shared prayer, whether read or spontaneous, draws one closer to Christ. A call out to God during times of physical or emotional pain becomes especially important.

This ministry of being with those in difficult situations, especially those actively dying, is called the "ministry of presence." It is described as "being" vs. "doing." It means we are grounded in the belief that Christ goes before us. When we can listen through the pain or suffering, and they will feel our sincere concern for them, trust is built. To be able to trust brings hope. When we know God's presence, we can more easily place our trust and hope in Christ. This can reduce anxiety and frequently pain and discomfort. Especially in the last weeks or days of one's life, it is helpful for the family to have a visitor who is known and trusted to sit with their loved one to give to them a break.

Rev. Marsha R. Jacobs writes in "Death is not the Enemy— Why End of Life Issues Should Matter in Churches"[13]: "This is the love that we as congregations demonstrate while being present with people as they live their lives and as they transition from this life to the next. We need to prepare each other more effectively for the end of life. I believe that the greatest gift we can give to those who love us is to let them know what our wishes are as to how we want our bodies treated as we near the end of our life."

Henri Nouwen writes about the ministry of presence. "I wonder more and more if the first thing shouldn't be to know people by name, to eat and drink with them, to listen to their stories and tell

---

[12] Karen Hardecopf, RN, "Ministry of Presence," *Parish Nurse Newsletter*-Lutheran Church, Missouri Synod, Fall 2017.

[13] Marsha R. Jacobs, "Death is not the Enemy—Why End of Life Issues Should Matter in Churches," *Church Health,* Fall 2011.

your own, and to let them know with words, handshakes, and hugs that you do not simply like them, but truly love them."[14]

"The Peace of God"
By Sue L. Frymark

I saw the "Presence of God" today.
It was in the eyes of a young woman who was dying,
Dying only in the physical sense,
For as she emotionally was maturing, the Spirit within her was permeating her presence.
Although her body was weakening and her discomforts increasing, she calmly laid
there telling me with her eyes, "I'm OK, Sue; I am OK."
The air was filled with the peaceful countenance of God, surrounding us as if He was holding us in His embrace.
As I left Darci's side for the last time, the joy within her soul was evident in her goodbye smile and gleaming eyes.
Darci was OK! Thanks be to God.

---

[14] Henri J. M. Nouwen, *Gracias!: A Latin American Journal* (Harper & Row, May 1, 1983), 148.

APPENDIX 1
Wilderness Journey Ministries

 Wilderness Journey Ministries Inc.

The authors decided the best way to apply their training and experience to problems people experience when living with a life-threatening illness was to create an educational support group. They developed a nine-week course they named "Help for Families: Facing a Life-Threatening Illness Holding Christ's Hand." They began teaching it in 2010 around the Portland, Oregon, area encouraging both the ill person and his or her family members to come together whenever possible. Over the next several years, they developed and self-published a participant's manual, a leader's guide, a training manual, and several videos.

The 108-page participant's manual offers practical, emotional, and spiritual advice. It is filled with scripture, devotionals, at-home lessons, and encouraging testimonies. Sometimes people find it impossible to attend nine weeks due to treatments schedules, work requirements, vacation plans, etc. To accommodate these people, the "Help for Families" material was broken down into three three-week segments called "Journeys." These can be scheduled at separate times as needed.

The leader's guide is comprehensive, offering suggestions, additional materials for various participants, and suggested handouts. The subject matter is complex enough that some experience is desirable. Training material is available if that is determined to be helpful. For more information, go to https://wjministries.org/.

Syllabus of Help for Families:

Journey 1—Starting the Conversation

Session 1: A Life-threatening Illness is a Family Experience
Key Concepts

- Overview
- A terminal diagnosis affects the whole family dramatically
- Terminal illness causes special difficulties
- Life changes forever
- The Lord is with you, holding your hand

Session 2: Coping with a Terminal Illness
Key Concepts

- Common emotions
- Special problems caused by terminal illnesses
- Good communication is important
- How to ask for help

Session 3: Planning for the Future
Key Concepts

- Important steps to take/documents to identify
- Modifying your environment to accommodate physical changes
- Searching for resources
- Settle unfinished business

- Advance Directives, POLST, and wills
- Planning the funeral

Journey 2—Where is God in the Turmoil?

Session 4: Living with Change
Key Concepts

- How children react
- Learning a new normal
- Focus on wellness
- Taking care of the caregiver
- Don't let the disease define who you are

Session 5: Dealing with the Why
Key Concepts

- Why is this happening to you?
- Where is God in all of this?
- What are the biblical explanations for suffering?
- Christ understands your suffering.

Session 6: Heaven and Other Things
Key Concepts

- About Heaven
- Will we get new bodies?
- About crowns
- About Judgment Day
- About Hell

Journey 3—A Time of Healing

Session 7: Difficult Decisions
Key Concepts

- Continuing treatment or stopping
- Palliative care/hospice
- Inpatient hospice/hospital
- The use of pain medication
- When to choose more treatment, when to stop
- Keeping in home or moving to another setting
- The right-to-die from a biblical perspective
- Deciding when to stop life support

Session 8: Later Stages
Key Concepts

- Preparing for the end
- Fear of death—blessed assurance
- The physical aspects of dying
- Keeping the vigil
- Bringing the family together
- Saying goodbye

Session 9: Eternal Purpose
Key Concepts

- The answer to the question of why
- A terminal illness can change the family forever
- God's symphony orchestra in the last days
- Passing the blessing
- What does your unique journey look like?
- How has God touched your family?

APPENDIX 2

Some Promises of God

From the King James Version:

Ps 9:9: The LORD also will be a refuge for the oppressed, a refuge in times of trouble.

Ps 22:24: For he hath not despised nor abhorred the affliction of the afflicted; neither hath he hid his face from him; but when he cried unto him, he heard.

Ps 27:14: Wait on the LORD: be of good courage, and he shall strengthen thine heart: wait, I say, on the LORD.

Ps 29:11: The LORD will give strength unto his people; the LORD will bless his people with peace.

Ps 34:17: The righteous cry, and the LORD heareth, and delivereth them out of all their troubles.

Ps 34:19: Many are the afflictions of the righteous: but the LORD delivereth him out of them all.

Ps 37:4–5: Delight thyself also in the LORD; and he shall give thee the desires of thine heart. Commit thy way unto the *LORD*; trust also in him; and he shall bring it to pass.

Ps 37:39–40: But the salvation of the righteous is of the LORD: he is their strength in the time of trouble. And the LORD shall help them and deliver them: he shall deliver them from the wicked and save them.

Ps 46:1: God is our refuge and strength, a very present help in trouble.

Is 40:29: He giveth power to the faint; and to them that have no might he increaseth strength.

Is 40:31: But they that wait upon the LORD shall renew their strength; they shall mount up with wings as eagles; they shall run, and not be weary; and they shall walk, and not faint.

Phil 4:7: And the peace of God, which passeth all understanding, shall keep your hearts and minds through Christ Jesus.

Ps 32:8: I will instruct thee and teach thee in the way which thou shalt go: I will guide thee with mine eye.

Ps 50:15: And call upon me in the day of trouble: I will deliver thee, and thou shalt glorify me.

Is 41:10: Fear thou not; for I am with thee: be not dismayed; for I am thy God: I will strengthen thee; yea, I will help thee; yea, I will uphold thee with the right hand of my righteousness.

Is 41:13: For I the LORD thy God will hold thy right hand, saying unto thee, Fear not; I will help thee.

Jer 29:13: And ye shall seek me, and find me, when ye shall search for me with all your heart.

Jer 33:3: Call unto me, and I will answer thee, and shew thee great and mighty things, which thou knowest not.

Mt 6:31–33: Therefore take no thought, saying, What shall we eat? or, What shall we drink? or, Wherewithal shall we be clothed? (For after all these things do the Gentiles seek): for your heavenly Father knoweth that ye have need of all these things. But seek ye first the kingdom of God, and his righteousness; and all these things shall be added unto you.

Mt 11:28–29: Come unto me, all ye that labour and are heavy laden, and I will give you rest. Take my yoke upon you, and learn of me; for I am meek and lowly in heart: and ye shall find rest unto your souls.

Mt 17:20: If ye have faith as a grain of mustard seed, ye shall say unto this mountain, remove hence to yonder place; and it shall remove; and nothing shall be impossible unto you.

Lk 11:9–10: And I say unto you, ask, and it shall be given you; seek, and ye shall find; knock, and it shall be opened unto you. For every one that asketh receiveth; and he that seeketh findeth; and to him that knocketh it shall be opened.

Jn 5:24: He that heareth my word, and believeth on him that sent me, hath ever-lasting life, and shall not come into condemnation; but is passed from death unto life.

Jn 14:18 I will not leave you comfortless: I will come to you.

Jn 14:27: Peace I leave with you, my peace I give unto you: not as the world giveth, give I unto you. Let not your heart be troubled, neither let it be afraid.

Jn 15:7: If ye abide in me, and my words abide in you, ye shall ask what ye will, and it shall be done unto you.

Jn 5:24: I tell you the truth, whoever hears my word and believes him who sent me has eternal life and will not be condemned; he has crossed over from death to life.

Jn 10:28: I give them eternal life, and they shall never perish; no one can snatch them out of my hand.

Is 41:10: So do not fear, for I am with you; do not be dismayed, for I am your God. I will strengthen you and help you; I will uphold you with my righteous right hand.

Heb 13:5–6 God has said, Never will I leave you; never will I forsake you. So we say with confidence, The Lord is my helper; I will not be afraid. What can man do to me?

Phil 4:6–7: Do not be anxious about anything, but in everything, by prayer and petition, with thanksgiving, present your requests to God. And the peace of God, which transcends all understanding, will guard your hearts and your minds in Christ Jesus.

Ps 32:8: I will instruct you and teach you in the way you should go; I will counsel you and watch over you.

Mt 11:28: Come to me, all you who are weary and burdened, and I will give you rest.

ABOUT THE AUTHORS

Karen Haren, Ph.D.

Karen has over 20 years' experience as lay prayer pastor, counselor, hospice worker, Stephen Minister, and program director. Karen did her undergraduate work at Pitzer College, majoring in psychology. After completing a master's in Applied Systems Management, she started her 17-year career in Telecommunications. The death of both her parents in 2003 opened her eyes to the very difficult journey so many people experience. She decided to take early retirement to go back to school and learn more about how to help. She attended Trinity College of the Bible and Theological Seminary and completed her Ph.D. in Biblical Counseling. She wrote her dissertation on how Christians can make biblically founded end-of-life decisions. Karen is also a Certified Christian Life and Bereavement Coach.

Sue Frymark, R.N. B.S. Retired

Sue is a graduate of Columbia School of Nursing in Milwaukee WI and earned her Bachelor of Science in Healthcare Administration from Concordia University. She focused her 30-year career on cancer care and hospice. Sue was the first nurse in Oregon trained in Hospice Care by Marin County Hospice in 1977. She continued to help establish hospice in Oregon as well as to develop a nationally known program of Cancer Rehabilitation. This interdisciplinary team helped people through all phases of cancer. The teams early training came from the pioneers of hospice and palliative care, Dame Cicely Saunders PHD, MD from St. Christopher's Hospice London England; as well as Dr. Belfour Mount of the Montreal Royal Victoria Hospital's Palliative Care Program. Sue received many awards and became nationally known for her contributions to Cancer Rehabilitation, hospice care, quality of life and end-of-life awareness, and program development. As a Christian, Sue felt the burden of not being able to share her faith with her patients. She could see the difference in the ability to cope between those with a strong faith and those with none.

Now retired, Sue spends her time with family and is active with her church, Faithful Savior Lutheran Church as a Stephen Ministry Leader and coordinator of Health Ministries. She has been a Master Trainer in "Powerful Tools for Caregivers" and "Living Well with a Chronic Illness."

Printed in the United States
By Bookmasters